NOTES
FOR
INFANTRY OFFICERS
ON
TRENCH WARFARE.

Compiled by the General Staff.

War Office,
March, 1916.

The Naval & Military Press Ltd

Published by the
The Naval & Military Press

Unit 10 Ridgewood Industrial Park,
Uckfield, East Sussex, TN22 5QE
Tel: +44 (0) 1825 749494
Fax: +44 (0) 1825 765701

MILITARY HISTORY AT YOUR FINGERTIPS
www.naval-military-press.com

ONLINE GENEALOGY RESEARCH
www.military-genealogy.com

ONLINE MILITARY CARTOGRAPHY
www.militarymaproom.com

In reprinting in facsimile from the original, any imperfections are inevitably reproduced and the quality may fall short of modern type and cartographic standards.

CONTENTS.

CHAP. I.—SPECIAL CHARACTERISTICS OF TRENCH WARFARE.

Sec.		Page
1	Trench fighting only a phase of war	5
2	Considerations affecting design of defences	5
3	Nature of field defences	7
4	The offensive spirit in trench warfare	8
5	Training in night work	8
6	Discipline	9
7	Training of specialists	9

CHAP. II.—SITING AND CONSTRUCTION OF TRENCHES.

8	Deliberate siting of trenches	10
9	Siting of trenches in the presence of the enemy	12
10	Concealment	13
11	Buildings	14
12	Woods	14
13	General description of a line of trenches	15
14	Strong points and defended localities	17
15	Defences in rear of the front system	18
16	Procedure when constructing trenches in the presence of the enemy	19
17	Constructional details of trenches	17
	Fire trenches	17
	Breastworks	23
	Loopholes	25
	Overhead cover	25
	Support trenches	25
	Communication trenches	25
18	Obstacles	27
19	Protection from shell fire	28
20	Machine gun emplacements	30
21	Latrines	31
22	Drainage and flooring	31
23	Defence of buildings	32
24	Training in digging, &c.	33

CHAP. III.—OCCUPATION AND RELIEF OF TRENCHES AND GENERAL TRENCH ROUTINE.

25	System of relief of trenches	34
26	Description of method of carrying out a relief	35
27	Precautions and arrangements necessary during a relief	36
28	Handing over trenches	37
29	Duties in trenches	37
30	Usual routine in trenches	39
31	Work in trenches	40
32	Observation and sniping	41
33	Co-operation with artillery	44
34	Sanitation and care of feet	45
35	Communications	46
36	Reports	47

CHAP. IV.—ORGANIZATION OF A TRENCH LINE AND ACTION
IN CASE OF ATTACK.

Sec.		Page
37	General considerations	48
38	Distribution of men in trenches	49
39	Machine guns	49
40	Action in case of attack	52
41	Action of artillery in case of attack	54

CHAP. V.—NOTES ON THE ATTACK IN TRENCH WARFARE.

42	Need for careful preparation	56
43	Infantry preparation for attack	56
44	Equipment	59
45	Preliminary bombardment	59
46	The assault	59
47	Action of artillery during the assault	60
48	Employment of machine guns	62
49	Use of grenadiers	62
50	Communications	63

APPENDIX A.—Breastwork Communication Trenches.	64
APPENDIX B.—Rapid Wire Entanglements.	68
APPENDIX C.—Illumination of Obstacles and Foreground.	69
APPENDIX D.—Infantry and Artillery Inter-Communication.	71

FIGURES AND DIAGRAMS.

Fig
1 Arrangement of Defensive Line.
2 Diagram of Supervision, Fire, and Communication Trenches.
3 Diagram of a Section of a Front Line with Supervision Trench, Dug-outs, and Shell Trenches.
4 Alternative Organization of a Front Line.
5 Type of Strong Point for 50 Men.
6 Supporting or Strong Point.
7, 8 Types of Fire Trenches.
9 Type of Bombing Pit with Protection.
10 Communication Trench Prepared for Fire.
11, 12 Method of Designing Straight Lengths of Communication Trench for Protection against Bombing.
13 Type of Sunk Wire Entanglement.
14 Wire Entanglement.
15 "Knife Rest."
16 Types of Dug-out Frames.
17 Type of Concreted Dug-out.
18–22 Types of Machine Gun Emplacements.
23–27 Breastwork Communication Trench.
28–32 Methods of putting up Rapid Entanglement.
33, 34 Automatic flare light and pit.

INDEX

NOTES FOR INFANTRY OFFICERS ON TRENCH WARFARE.

CHAPTER I.

SPECIAL CHARACTERISTICS OF TRENCH WARFARE.

1. *Trench Fighting only a Phase of Warfare.*

The importance assumed by trench warfare and the progress made in the application of field fortification and in the science of the attack and defence of elaborate systems of trenches, have rendered necessary special instruction in the details of trench construction and trench fighting. It must, nevertheless, be clearly understood that trench fighting is only a phase of operations, and that instruction in this subject, essential as it is, is only one branch of the training of troops. To gain a decisive success the enemy must be driven out of his defences and his armies crushed in the open.

The aim of trench fighting is, therefore, to create a favourable situation for field operations, which the troops must be capable of turning to account.

2. *Considerations affecting Design of Defences.*

1. Three facts in particular give to modern trench fighting under present conditions most of its special characteristics. These are—

(a) The continual proximity of the opposing forces;
(b) The length of time for which they have generally occupied the same ground;
(c) The fact that neither side has a flank so long as it remains on the defensive, so that every attack must be frontal.

2. As a result of the length of time the opposing forces have been in close proximity on practically the same ground, the original trenches dug at the end of a period of manœuvre operations have grown into a complicated system of entrenchments. The design and organization of these have been influenced by the nature of

the artillery, up to calibres far heavier than could be utilised in ordinary field operations, which the stationary nature of the fighting has made it possible to bring up. Arrangements have been made by a carefully thought out system of inter-communication for the maximum co-operation between artillery and infantry, both in attack and defence, and artillery has had time to register on all targets within range. Thus either side has it in its power to concentrate heavy fire at very short notice upon any selected target, and to maintain that fire for a length of time which difficulties of ammunition supply would put out of the question in manœuvre operations. Consequently, the rapidity with which artillery can form a barrage to meet attack makes it necessary that the moment of the assault should come as a surprise, and the trenches from which an attack is to be made should therefore be within close assaulting distance of the opposing front line.

3. A system of trenches must therefore be designed which facilitates the preparation and launching of an unexpected assault, and at the same time is adapted to meet a sudden attack by the enemy. The organization of a trench system to facilitate attack is an important point, which is frequently neglected. If additional trenches have to be hastily made when an attack is intended, the intention to attack will be obvious to the enemy by aerial reconnaissance, and surprise will be out of the question.

4. Modern field fortifications owe their elaborate form to the means employed in attack and defence respectively. A general idea of what those means are is therefore necessary.

The aim of the first stages of attack is to obtain a footing in the enemy's defences and to consolidate and extend the gain thus made. Penetration is effected by means of an infantry assault, which, as has been said, must unavoidably be frontal and depends for success on a certain measure of surprise.

The infantry attack may be assisted by any or all of the following methods :—

(a) The previous destruction, by bombardment or explosion of mines or a combination of both, of the enemy's material defences, including obstacles ;

(b) The shaking of the moral and destruction of the *personnel* of the defending force by bombardment or by the employment of one of the new agents of war, such as asphyxiating gas or jets of liquid fire, prior to assault ;

(c) Keeping down hostile fire over the area to be crossed by the attacking infantry long enough to enable the assaulting troops to reach the cover of the enemy's defences ;

(d) The isolation, by artillery barrages, of the area to be assaulted, so as to prevent the arrival of reinforcements ;

(e) The dispersal or destruction of troops collecting for counter-attack.

5. To meet these measures the defence employs the following means :—

(a) Constant close observation, with a view to the detection of any signs of impending attack ;*
(b) Concentration of fire on any detected assembly which might be the prelude to assault ;
(c) Concentration of fire of artillery, machine guns, and rifles, from as wide a front as possible, over any part of the zone lying between the two lines, so as to prevent the penetration of the defence ;
(d) Obstacles to delay the assaulting troops as long as possible under this fire ;
(e) Barrages of fire to prevent the reinforcement of, or the sending up of materials, ammunition, or supplies to, any body of troops that has succeeded in penetrating the defence ;
(f) Disposition of works so as to localise and confine the effect of penetration at any point ;†
(g) Destruction by artillery fire of any enemy troops that have penetrated ;
(h) Immediate counter-attack, to drive out the attackers before they can have recovered from the confusion of the assault and have established themselves securely in the captured area.

3. *Nature of Field Defences.*

A consideration of the above shows that there are certain features which are essential in a system of trenches. They must be strong, to resist heavy bombardment ; they must be sited and designed to favour, by the utilization of oblique and enfilade fire of rifles and, above all, of machine guns, the development of the maximum volume of fire over any part of their front ; they must be protected by a strong and well hidden wire entanglement, in order to retain attacking infantry under this fire ; they must provide protection for the garrison against weather and against the effect of artillery fire. Fire and shelter trenches must be numerous in order to accommodate the additional troops to be placed in them previous to an attack on the enemy's line, and also, in the defence, to induce dispersion of hostile artillery fire, to permit the temporary withdrawal of the garrison from a heavily shelled zone, and to accommodate troops for local counter-attack in close proximity to the points where they may be required. Communications must be ample, to admit of the rapid re-occupation of temporarily evacuated trenches, to minimise the interference of hostile fire with reinforcement and supply, and to facilitate local counter-attack. Close observation of the enemy must be provided for by listening posts in advance of the front line and by observing stations in or behind it. Finally, the system of trenches must admit of immediate

---
* *E.g.*, instalment of gas apparatus, advance of saps, passages cut in enemy's wire to facilitate egress.
† See Sections 14, 15.

readjustment of the front, so that the effect of penetration at any point may be localised and need not weaken the hold of the defence on adjacent trenches.

4. *The Offensive Spirit in Trench Warfare.*

The attack on such a system of defences as has been described demands in all ranks dash and gallantry of a very high order, and in the subordinate leader, down to the lowest grades, a quick perception, rapid decision, and intelligent initiative. It is more than ever the case that success depends upon qualities of leadership in subordinate commanders, upon rapid appreciation and readiness to accept responsibility on the part of the man on the spot. Much can be done in peace training to foster these qualities and to impress on even the most subordinate leaders the necessity for acting, in cases of urgency, on their own responsibility. At the same time, the state of comparative inactivity, which is the normal condition of life in the trenches, is very unfavourable to the development of these qualities in officers and men. There is an insidious tendency to lapse into a passive and lethargic attitude, against which officers of all ranks have to be on their guard, and the fostering of the offensive spirit, under such unfavourable conditions, calls for incessant attention. Minor local enterprises and constant occupation during the tour of duty in the trenches furnish the best means of maintaining the efficiency of the troops. The repair, maintenance, and improvement of the trenches furnish ample work to afford employment to the troops, who must be made to understand that this work reacts in their own favour in the shape of increased security and comfort and conditions more favourable to health. Constant activity in harassing the enemy may lead to reprisals at first, and for this reason is sometimes neglected, but, if persevered in, it always results in an ultimate mastery, it gives the troops a healthy interest and wholesome topics of conversation, and it achieves the double purpose of raising the moral of our own troops whilst lowering that of the enemy's. Every effort should be made to obtain the mastery over the enemy's snipers.

5. *Training in Night-work.*

The proximity of the opposing lines, the progress of aerial reconnaissance, and the close and continuous watch which either side maintains over the other, have increased the importance of night-work. Many of the daily operations incidental to trench warfare can only be carried out under cover of darkness. The construction of new trenches in sight of the enemy, and much of their maintenance and repair, the construction, repair, and improvement of obstacles, and in many cases the bringing up of materials and stores and the relief of the garrison, cannot be carried out by daylight. The assembly of troops and many of the final stages of preparation for an attack, as, for instance, the removal of our own obstacles, can only be kept from the enemy's knowledge by carrying them out at night. The close reconnaissance of the enemy's front line and his obstacles and of the ground to be crossed by an assault is the work of night patrols, and much of the identification of the troops opposed to us—a very important duty—can only be effected by small enterprises carried out by night against the enemy's patrols or listening posts, or sometimes against a small section of his trenches. Training in all these branches of night-work is an important part of the instruction of troops before leaving for the front.

6. *Discipline.*

The hardships, discomfort, and dangers of life in the trenches make great demands upon the endurance of the troops; the frontal attack on an enemy in a position strengthened and defended by every device that ingenuity and forethought can conceive calls for exceptional resolution and determination, and the defence of trenches against an attack, preluded generally by a protracted and severe bombardment, and often by the employment of some entirely new and unforeseen agency, requires the utmost steadfastness and devotion. No infantry will possess those qualities to the requisite degree that has not a very high standard of discipline. The first and greatest aim of all training should therefore be the establishment of the strictest discipline. To attain this there is no other method than constant and precise drill, strict enforcement of march discipline, insistence on a rigid exactness in the performance of even the dullest details of camp and barrack routine, and unceasing attention to apparently trifling detail in time of training. Without such previous preparation the silent and thorough execution of work and performance of duties, in darkness and in danger, in the presence of the enemy, and often without direct supervision of a superior, which distinguish good from bad troops and spell success, are impossible of attainment.

7. *Training of Specialists.*

The present type of warfare in the trenches has involved the training of a proportion of men in infantry units in duties of a special nature, *e.g.*, grenade-throwing, pioneer work, sniping, &c.

A word of warning is necessary as regards the training of these men. They must be made to realise that their training in these special duties is *in addition to* their ordinary training as infantry soldiers and must not be allowed to interfere with their performance of the ordinary duties of infantry soldiers, except when they are required for the special duties in which they have been trained.

CHAPTER II.

SITING AND CONSTRUCTION OF TRENCHES.

8. *Deliberate Siting of Trenches.*

1. The problem of selecting the position of fire trenches varies according to the circumstances under which the choice has to be made and the work carried out. The siting and construction of a trench line in the presence of the enemy and under fire is influenced by factors which are absent in the deliberate and undisturbed choice such as can be made when preparing a rear line. It is important to recognise that the two problems are distinct, and that their solution calls for different methods.

2. The first step in the case of a line which is to be constructed free from interference by the enemy, and under circumstances which make time a factor of minor importance, is a deliberate reconnaissance of the ground. This reconnaissance will usually consist of two stages. The first deals with the problem on broad lines, compares the merits of alternative general solutions, determines the general line to be taken up, and lays down certain points or localities as having special importance and calling for special treatment. Following on this, a second, more detailed, reconnaissance is made, in which are considered the form of the works to be constructed for the defence of the tactical features and localities laid down in the general scheme, and the method of treating the intervals between these strong points or localities. As a result of this detailed reconnaissance, large scale plans are produced showing the exact siting and constructional detail of the essential works. The decision as to the general line to be taken up is the business of the General Staff of the formation (division, corps or army) concerned. The Chief Engineer Officer will advise as to the constructional details of the line selected. In both stages of the reconnaissance due weight should be given to the questions of facilities for attack, and of securing good observation for ourselves and denying it to the enemy, cohesion in defence by mutual support of adjoining works, drainage and concealment; the final decision arrived at is a balance between the often conflicting requirements of these different considerations. The order of importance of the works is another point decided in the two stages of the reconnaissance. Not until the reconnaissance has been completed should any work be begun, and, although the close study of the ground during the execution of the works will probably suggest improvements in detail—in fact, a good deal of the detail should be left to be elaborated at this stage—it will seldom be necessary or advisable to alter any of the essential

features, determined by the reconnaissance, during the construction of the defences.

3. Unless the ground is almost absolutely flat, the most important question in siting trenches is whether to occupy the tops of the hills, establishing the front line trenches on either the crest or the forward slope, or to withdraw the main front line to the reverse slope, taking up what is known as the "back" or "retired" position. The chief argument advanced in favour of this latter position is that it affords greater security against hostile artillery fire. Now it must be borne in mind that the question of protection from artillery fire, so far as it is affected by siting, is almost entirely one of security from observation. Any target can be heavily and accurately engaged if fire on it can be effectively observed from a point in the occupation of the force which is carrying out the bombardment. The position of the observer relative to the gun is immaterial, that of the target to the gun position almost equally so. If either side is in occupation of the hill-tops, and can establish an artillery officer with a telescope and a telephone on the high ground, its facilities for observation of fire are greater than those of its opponent, situated lower down the slopes. That being the case, the "back position" loses the advantage of protection from artillery fire claimed for it, unless we can deny to the enemy's observers the use of the high ground. Experience has shown that, except in the case of isolated features of small extent, when a concentration of fire may effect the desired purpose, the only effective way to deny ground to the enemy is to occupy it oneself.

Front line trenches on the crest or forward slope are certainly exposed to view and therefore to bombardment, though this is not so much the case as it would be if the enemy were looking down on them, and the disadvantage can be diminished by adequate provision of material protection for the garrison. On the other hand, the occupation of the high ground gives a feeling of superiority which reacts favourably on the moral of the troops. Only those who have experienced it can appreciate the depressing effect produced by the feeling of discomfort and inferiority of position under which troops suffer, who have to occupy for some time trenches looked down upon by those of the enemy. The forward position has the further advantage, if the front line is not dug too far down the forward slope, that supporting trenches, communications, and the works in which a large proportion of the garrison live, enjoy a comparative immunity from observation. In offensive action the forward position offers greater facilities for observation, on which the effectiveness of the previous preparation by bombardment largely depends, and for the assembly of troops for the assault, close to the front line and unobserved.

4. Special conditions may justify the deliberate choice of the "retired" position. If it is adopted, arrangements must be made to deny the enemy access to the crest of the hill, and to secure it for ourselves. The front trench line must not be too far below

the crest line—50 to 100 yards will usually be far enough and is a sufficient field of fire if machine guns are well sited—and there must be an ample number of saps forward to the top to allow of continuous observation of the forward slope. With these precautions, and readiness to deliver an immediate and vigorous counter-attack on the enemy if he appears on the crest, the back position may sometimes be taken up when conditions impose a temporarily defensive attitude and the local superiority in artillery is with the enemy. But if the two lines remain facing one another on the same ground for a protracted period it will be impossible to prevent the enemy indefinitely from establishing himself on the crest unless it is included in our line.

5. In deciding on both the general and the detailed trace of the line a common tendency, which is to be avoided, is towards making it too straight. An irregular line, with frequent salients and re-entrants, gives greater facilities for concentration of fire over any desired area and for the most effective employment of machine guns. It will expose short lengths of trench to enfilade fire, but suitable construction will minimise the effect of this. In any case the effect is generally reciprocal ; from a salient in our line some part of the enemy's line pushed forward into the adjoining re-entrant will be exposed to our enfilade fire. These remarks apply with almost equal force to a large salient, constructed to include an important tactical point, and to minor irregularities in the trace of trenches. The latter should be made as a matter of invariable principle. The former should be used boldly where circumstances demand them. The determining considerations in their case are two :—

(a) Whether the possession of the point in question by us would facilitate future offensive action without unduly weakening our line ;

(b) Whether its possession by the enemy would seriously threaten the security of our trenches.

9. *Siting of Trenches in the Presence of the Enemy.*

1. The presence of the enemy will frequently make it impossible to select the position of fire trenches entirely on the merits of the ground. Their site will often be decided by the chance and accident of close fighting, and their general position will coincide roughly with the high-water mark reached for the moment by the attack. Troops who are unable to make any further advance will either occupy a hostile trench which has been captured in the course of the attack or start at once to procure for themselves what cover they can with the tools at their disposal, generally, for the most part, only the entrenching tool. Much can be done by officers at this stage in the way of small adjustments of position and of the distribution of their men with a view to the future development of the hasty cover constructed into the best line that circumstances will admit. Unless this is done, much of the work

may be found afterwards to be useless, valuable time and effort will have been wasted, and troops may either have to try and hold an unfavourable position or be exposed again in the construction of a fresh one. Serious work will generally be impossible before dusk, unless arrangements can be made for a heavy covering fire, and after dusk it is difficult to avoid mistakes in the choice and siting of a line. Every officer, then, who finds his command unable to make further progress, should take advantage of the daylight to study the ground as far as circumstances permit, and should make up his mind exactly what line he will take up if forced to dig himself in.

2. The main problem that arises in this case is whether any of the ground won should be abandoned in order to secure a more suitable line of defence. Generally, if the check is merely temporary and it is intended to resume the advance at the earliest opportunity, all ground gained should be held except for very minor adjustments, unless some portion is clearly untenable against counter-attack ; if, however, strategical or tactical considerations require a temporary abandonment of the forward movement and the construction of a defensive line to be held for some time, the decision will be governed to a great extent by the same considerations as already discussed in taking up a line deliberately, and it may be advisable to give up ground on some parts of the front.

3. The satisfactory siting of a trench line constructed in these circumstances will largely depend on the power possessed by the officers on the spot to recognise during the various stages of a battle the minor features of real tactical importance. The ability to recognise these is only acquired by previous training, and is a quality which every officer must study to possess.

10. *Concealment.*

The development of aerial reconnaissance has made concealment of a *position* impossible, but isolated works and gun emplacements can be hidden, and trenches in a wood may remain undetected if clearing is not overdone. But aerial observers can not only invariably locate trenches in open country but can obtain photographs showing every trench and every traverse. Good aeroplane photographs show even the wire entanglements. This is not to be interpreted as meaning that no attention need be paid to the question of concealment. Anything that tends to make a trench less conspicuous and increases the difficulty of observing fire on it for an observer on the ground is of value. If natural cover is turned to account, the existence of a trench at a particular spot may not be detected at once and it may escape the attentions of the enemy's artillery at the stage when it is most vulnerable. In siting trenches with a view to concealment the hiding of the wire entanglements and supervision and communication trenches must not be overlooked. Tracks and much trampled ground show up very clearly from the air, and may draw attention to an otherwise well hidden work. Work done to buildings themselves is easily concealed from aerial reconnaissance, but the existence of trenches round or leading into a building gives a clear indication of its occupation.

The fact that trenches cannot be concealed from aerial observation makes it most important that every system of trenches should be so designed that an attack can be made from them without the necessity of constructing fresh trenches at the last moment, which would give away the fact that an attack was intended. · Airmen cannot see whether a trench is occupied or not without coming down dangerously low.

11. *Buildings.*

It will frequently happen that substantial buildings are found close to the selected line of defence. The question then arises whether to occupy them or to demolish them. The decision will depend generally upon two points, whether they have cellars which can be improved into good cover, and whether it is possible to demolish them. Buildings in or near the front line invariably draw a lot of fire from artillery, and unless good cover can be contructed in connection with them are nothing but shell traps. Solid blocks of buildings, on the other hand, with cellars which can be improved to give good cover against bombardment have on many occasions proved very difficult to take. Buildings of this nature had better be included in the line if possible, as they can be converted into strong points, and if left to be occupied by the enemy might prove both a thorn in the flesh to the defence and an obstacle to attack. A building which has no cellars may be left out of the line if it can be effectively demolished so as to afford no cover to the enemy. Effective demolition is a technical job which requires the co-operation of the R.E. and demands a certain amount of time. Where it is neither possible to carry out an effective demolition, nor desirable to distort the line so as to include a building or a group of buildings, these may sometimes be held as an advanced post to prevent their occupation by the enemy. In this case they must be connected up with the main line by communication trenches and special measures to deal at the shortest possible notice with a sudden enterprise must be arranged.

12. *Woods.*

1. A position in a wood affords a certain amount of concealment from observation. It is easy to conceal the wire entanglement so that accurate artillery fire cannot be brought to bear on it. If the position of the line taken up is such that the enemy can establish himself inside the wood he will enjoy similar advantages. Therefore, where there is freedom of choice, the best line to take up is one which secures cover from observation for ourselves, whilst denying the edge of the wood to the enemy. The exact distance

inside the wood of this position cannot be definitely laid down, but experience has shown that 30 to 50 yards from the front edge usually provides ample concealment from observation. Under no circumstances should the front edge itself be occupied, as hostile artillery can obtain the range of it with accuracy. Breastworks with a parados are generally more suitable in a wood than trenches ; in either case the space between parapet and parados should be made as narrow as possible to keep down casualties from splinters of shell bursting in the trees. Otherwise the siting and design of trenches in a wood do not call for any special observations.

2. If a wood cannot be included in the line and has to be left unoccupied in close proximity to it, special arrangements must be made for the concentration of fire on the near edge of the wood and on the ground between it and the front line trench, to deal with an attack by enemy who could assemble unseen under cover of the wood.

13. *General Description of a Line of Trenches.**

The front system of trenches comprises the front line and its support and reserve trenches. In front of the front line is an obstacle continuous except for narrow inconspicuous passages at intervals to serve as exits for reconnoitring patrols. The trenches may be constructed completely below ground, they may consist of a combination of trench and parapet, or the necessary cover may be provided entirely above ground level by the construction of breastworks. The first type is very seldom met with, while the use of breastworks is practically confined to positions where water makes them necessary and where time admits of their construction. The combination of trench and parapet is that most commonly met with, the depth of the trench being generally determined by the wetness of the site and facilities for drainage. The front line generally consists of two parts, the fire trench and the command or supervision trench. The fire trench may either be a continuous trench (though in no case should it be an absolutely straight one), traversed at suitable intervals to give protection from enfilade fire and to localise the effect of shell bursts, or may consist of fire bays, T-shaped or L-shaped in plan, jutting forward from the supervision trench. The latter is a continuous trench affording easy lateral communication close behind the fire bays or fire trench, and connected with them at frequent intervals. In the case of fire bays there must be a communication trench forward from the supervision trench to each bay. In the case of a continuous fire trench the best position for these communication trenches to come into the fire trench is behind a traverse, and there should be one such communication trench behind about every second traverse. (See figs. 2, 3, and 4.)

2. Emplacements for machine guns are constructed in the front

---

* See fig. 1.

line so that the whole front of the line can be swept with machine gun fire, which for the maximum effect should be from a flank across the front covered. It is, therefore, essential that the trace of a trench should not be straight. Machine guns can also often be effectively employed behind the front line in small inconspicuous emplacements, where they may escape detection and consequent bombardment prior to an attack. The question of machine gun emplacements must always receive most careful attention. (See Section 20.)

3. The support trenches (see Section 17 (7)) accommodate the first support to the garrison of the front trench, ready for immediate reinforcement or local counter-attack ; they also furnish cover to which the bulk of the garrison of the front trench can be temporarily withdrawn during bombardment.* The support line should always be constructed as a second line of resistance, if the first line is lost, and should be protected by an obstacle. The line of support trenches may or may not be continuous, it is preferable that it should be ; in any case it is connected to the front line by frequent communication trenches. In order that support trenches may not suffer from the bombardment of the front line they should not be nearer than 50 yards behind it, and the most favourable position is from 70 to 100 yards behind.

4. Behind the support trenches, and also connected with them by communication trenches, lies the reserve line, which may consist of a line of trenches but more usually of dug-outs, often formed by improving the cover afforded by some natural feature. The reserve trenches or dug-outs are to accommodate the battalion reserve, whose purpose is the local counter-attack. The reserve line may be from 400 to 600 yards in rear of the front line.

5. To the above are often added trenches made for a special purpose, e.g., a " bombing trench " (which is a trench dug behind the front line within easy grenade throwing distance of it, its purpose being to enable an enemy who has captured the front line to be driven out by grenades) or so-called " slit " trenches dug off the communication trenches for the accommodation of men during a bombardment. (See Section 19 (8) and fig. 3.)

6. A system of trenches is also usually provided with a series of works prepared for all round defence, and surrounded with a continuous obstacle, known variously as "keeps," "supporting points,"."strong points," or "reduits." Their object is to break up a hostile attack which has penetrated the front line and prevent its further development and thus to facilitate counter-attack. Their garrison must hold out to the last, whatever

---

* Under favourable circumstances the bulk of the garrison of the front line may normally be accommodated during the day in the support trenches, leaving the front line to be garrisoned by groups of sentries only. The question of the distribution of men in the trenches is discussed later in Chapter IV. The question of the provision and position of shelter against the weather and bombardment for the garrison of the fire and support trenches is discussed later in this chapter.

happens to the rest of the line. They must come as a surprise to the enemy, and, therefore, be carefully concealed. No definite rules can be laid down as to their number on a given frontage or their relative position with regard to the front line; this will usually depend on the facilities offered by the ground for their concealment. Adjacent works of this kind should, if possible, afford mutual support to one another.

7. Latrines are provided in all trenches, and must be in positions easy of access and protected from fire. They are usually made in T-heads at the end of short trenches leading off from the supervision trench.

Communication trenches are made to the front system from points on roads which can be reached without too much exposure to view.

14. *Strong Points and Defended Localities.*

1. In every line there will be a certain number of points of which the loss, or their occupation by the enemy, would seriously endanger the security of the rest of the line, or would weaken the defender's hold on it. There will also probably be other points which are particularly favourable for defence. Such points should receive special treatment so as to develop to the utmost their capabilities for defence, and to enable the troops to hold on to them even after the neighbouring portions of the line have been lost. In addition, if the intervals between them are great, there should be small intermediate works. The important thing about all these works is that they should be designed so as to be able to offer a protracted resistance, unsupported if necessary, to hostile attacks from any direction, flank and rear as well as frontal. The importance of the point to be strengthened, its position, and its nature generally determine the area to be embraced within the perimeter of the work. Speaking generally, large defended localities offer a less concentrated target to the enemy's guns, and are, therefore, less vulnerable, but they absorb large garrisons.

2. The small strong point referred to in last section is generally in the nature of an enclosed infantry redoubt with a continuous parapet round its whole perimeter, designed to be held by a garrison which may be anything from a section to half a company. The garrison should be kept as small as possible, and the defence provided by machine guns as far as possible. This type of work must be carefully concealed and strongly constructed, or it will become a "shell-trap." Good bomb-proof protection for its garrison should be provided within the perimeter of the work. (See fig. 5.)

3. The more important points are better defended by a system of trenches covering a more extended area, and forming what is better described as a defended locality. The perimeter of such a defended locality should be provided with defences against an attack from any direction, these defences consisting either of a

continuous fire trench, or of isolated lengths of fire trench sited to cover every possible line of approach, and connected with one another and with the works in the interior of the locality by communication trenches. Small self-contained works such as have been described in the last paragraph might quite well form an element in the defences of the perimeter or in the interior defences of a locality. Within the defended perimeter should be the dug-outs for the garrison and a series of cover and support trenches and communication trenches, many of them prepared for occupation as fire trenches. In this way the interior is cut up into compartments, and the scheme of defence is so organized that, even if the enemy succeeds in establishing a footing at some point in the perimeter, an unbroken front can still be presented to him, and the defender's hold on the locality is practically unaffected. Machine guns play an important part in the defence, and alternative emplacements should be numerous. The sitings of the emplacements should be very carefully considered, and will largely govern the general design of the defences. A defended locality of this nature has the advantage that it does not offer a concentrated artillery target, and that its reduction by bombardment would be a difficult and lengthy operation, entailing a large expenditure of ammunition.

4. Villages placed in a state of defence make the best kind of supporting point. If the defence is properly organized, their capture has usually proved a long and costly operation. Cellars, with their roofs shored up and reinforced, form excellent shelters, and good communications entirely underground can be made by breaking through from cellar to cellar. The organization of the defence will be similar to that already outlined for defended localities. The field of fire from interior lines of resistance must be improved wherever necessary by the thorough demolition of buildings and removal or spreading of the *debris*.

5. These strong points or localities should, as has been already stated, be provided with a good obstacle all round them. In addition, any interior trench which may, under the scheme of defence, at any time become a line of resistance, should also be covered by a wire entanglement.

6. Unity of command is an important thing in the defence of one of these works, and they should, with this in view, be designed for a garrison of a complete unit, as far as possible.

15. *Defences in Rear of the Front System.*

The defences in rear of the front system should consist of a zone 4 or 5 miles deep, in which all points of tactical importance are fortified on the principles laid down in Section 14. The intention is by the occupation of these points to break up the attack of any hostile force which has penetrated the front system, delay any further advance, and facilitate counter-attack. In addition to this primary role, these strong points furnish a framework on which, by digging trenches in the intervals, a new line within the zone can be rapidly constructed to meet any eventuality.

A second similar zone may be prepared in rear of the first.

16. *Procedure when Constructing Trenches in the Presence of the Enemy.*

1. The procedure in the case of constructing a line when hostile interference has not to be reckoned with has already been described. In the construction of a line in the presence of an enemy the first object is to get some sort of cover, as quickly as possible, for the firing line. Normally what happens is that individual men start to dig pits for themselves where they were when the advance stopped. As soon as possible these pits are joined up with one another to form a continuous fire trench. This trench may ultimately form the front fire trench, a continuous trench for purposes of lateral communication being subsequently dug behind it, or it may become the supervision trench, fresh fire trenches being pushed out at intervals from it to the front. In either case, but more especially in the former, much subsequent labour will be saved if the question of traverses in the final trench is taken into account, both in the spacing of the first constructed pits and in the joining of them up to form a trench (see details regarding traverses in Section 17). If it is decided to use the trench first formed as a supervision trench, the next stage, after it is completed, is that T-heads are pushed forward from it to form the firing bays. The work of digging the individual pits will be begun by the infantry with any tools they have, generally, as has been said, mostly with infantry entrenching tools. Troops must, therefore, be well practised in digging themselves in by night or day with these tools. But heavier tools must be got up to the firing line as soon as possible, and every plan for an advance should provide for a certain number of digging tools, other than the entrenching tool, accompanying the attack,* and for this number being supplemented as early as possible with every available pick and shovel. It may be necessary to wait for dark before a large quantity of tools can be brought up and serious work attempted, but it is sometimes possible, under covering fire from the artillery, to dig a continuous trench by day. In any case, every effort must be made to get good trenches dug as soon as possible. One of the first requirements is to get some wire in front of the trench, as this gives a greater feeling of security to the men digging (see Appendix B). During the first two or three days it may be expected that the new line will be subjected to heavy bombardment alternating with repeated counter-attacks. If the front

---

* See Chapter V.

trench is constructed in the first instance very close to the enemy's position it is particularly vulnerable to counter-attack and if the enemy succeeds in breaking through the line at a time when there are no defences prepared behind it, he may force a retirement on a large front. The construction of a supporting line 70 to 100 yards in rear of the front line and of a reserve line should, therefore, be proceeded with simultaneously.

2. The following procedure, adopted in at least one instance by the Germans, may commend itself when the offensive has to be temporarily given up, and the enemy is found established in a prepared line. A line is constructed in the first instance at a considerable distance, say 500 to 600 yards, or even more, from the the enemy's front trench, the exact distance depending on the ground and facilities in the form of cover. This line is made fairly strong and complete before any further advance is attempted. Then, under cover of night, and possibly of a heavy bombardment of the enemy's front line, a new front line is constructed at a distance of 200 to 300 yards from the enemy. From this point further advance would usually be by sap. The advantage of this method is that, before any attempt is made to dig a line within easy reach of small counter-attacks, there is a completed line ready behind the new line, to stop further progress by the enemy if the new line is counter-attacked and broken.

17. *Constructional Details of Trenches.*

1. *Fire Trenches.*—There is no sealed pattern of fire trench. Various types which have been found useful are shown in figs. 6 to 8, but the type used varies according to local conditions. Any fire trench, however, must fulfil the following essential conditions :—

(a) The parapet must be bullet-proof ;
(b) Every man must be able to fire *over* the parapet with proper effect (*i.e.*, so that he can hit the bottom of his own wire) ;
(c) Traverses must be adequate ;
(d) A parados must be provided to give protection against the back-blast of high explosive ;
(e) The trace of the trench should be irregular, to provide flanking fire ;

and, if the trench is to be held for any length of time :—

(f) The sides must be revetted ;
(g) The bottom of the trench must be floored.

The narrower a trench is the better the cover which it affords. However, a trench which may have to be occupied for some time must allow freedom of movement. The result is that a fire trench is usually made broad enough to allow of movement behind the line of men manning the parapet. Every man must be able to use his rifle over the parapet ; on the other hand people moving along the trench do not want to have to stoop down low in order to get their heads under the cover of the parapet. Therefore the trench usually has a firing step about 18 inches broad and 4 feet 6 inches below the crest of the parapet, and behind this a deeper portion from 18 inches to 2 feet 6 inches broad at the bottom and from 6 feet to 7 feet below the crest line of the parapet (see figs. 7, 8). The firing step must have a level surface and give a firm foothold. It may either consist of an earth step strongly revetted with planks held up by well driven pickets, or of stout planks laid on low timber trestles. Sandbags are sometimes used but are not suitable, as such a firing step gets very slippery in wet weather and usually takes a slope to the rear, so that it gives a very insecure foothold. Height from firing step to crest to be frequently tested. The only test is whether the individual man can use his rifle effectively over the top.

2. *Traverses.*—Traverses are strong buttresses of earth jutting out from the front or the rear face of the trench so as to split it into a series of compartments. Their object is to decrease the exposure of the garrison to enfilade fire and to localise the effect of a shell bursting in the trench. For both these purposes they must be strong and solid. They should be made from 9 to 12 feet thick, should overlap the width of the trench by 2 feet at least, and must be strongly revetted. A traverse is described as a "forward" traverse or a "rear" traverse according as it juts out from the back or the front face of the trench respectively. Rear traverses are generally accepted as the best for normal use, but an occasional forward traverse is useful to provide fire to a flank. Traverses add to the length of trench necessary to accommodate a given number of rifles, and, if they are too frequent, add to the difficulty of supervision and control. From 18 feet to 30 feet is the normal length of bay between two adjacent traverses. Traverses in a trench facilitate bombing attacks along its length, as grenades can be thrown from under cover of a traverse, generally into the next bay but one. As a protection against this there should be, at intervals in the line, spaces without traverses, long enough to prevent bombing from behind the traverse

at one end of the space to beyond the traverse at the other end. This length of trench should be straight and the traverses on either side of it should be loopholed for fire inwards. Bombing trenches or pits behind the front line (see figs. 3 and 9) are also useful to stop an attack of this sort.

Traverses will often have to be made in a completed trench which is insufficiently traversed. To do this cut into the face of the trench opposite that from which the traverse is to jut out a recess broad enough and deep enough for the end of the traverse and the passage round it, and with the earth from this recess, supplemented if necessary by more from elsewhere, build up a wall of sandbags or of earth revetted with sandbags or other material 9 feet to 12 feet thick right across the old trench and projecting not less than 2 feet into the recess. (See figure, p. 21.)

3. The sides of trenches which have to be occupied for a long time, and particularly in wet weather in a damp site, must be revetted. Hurdles or rabbit netting held up by stout stakes at frequent intervals, well driven and with their upper ends securely wired to short pickets firmly anchored in the parapet or parados, form a useful type of revetment for this purpose. Sandbags are not so suitable. High revetments in Flanders clay require an intermediate anchorage between the bottom of the revetment stake and the anchorage to its top, unless revetment stakes of 4 to 5 inches diameter are used. The placing of this in the solid ground forming the side of a trench is a difficult operation demanding the assistance of skilled labour. In the winter in Flanders some really solid form of revetment, such as planks or timber, or expanded metal sheets, is necessary.

The fire trench should be provided with frequent exits for the use of patrols. These exits should be in the form of tunnels leading under the parapet, whether the line be trench or breastwork, and communicating with saps.

The top of the parapet should always be irregular, as this helps to conceal men observing or firing over the parapet. Still better concealment is provided if the parados is higher than the parapet and is also irregular, as heads do not then show up against a skyline.

A useful accessory in a trench line is what is known as a "bombing trench" or "bombing pits." The latter are small recesses about 5 feet square dug behind the front line and within easy grenade throwing range of it (see fig. 9). The former is a continuous trench for the same purpose.

A tendency to be guarded against is that towards gradually increasing the width of trenches. Wide trenches are undoubtedly more comfortable to live in but they afford nothing like such good protection as narrower trenches. In repairing a trench of which the side has fallen in men are apt merely to throw the earth out which has fallen in. This should never be allowed; the débris should be cleared away, a strong revetment (hurdles, expanded metal or rabbit-netting) put up against the new face, and a sandbag wall built outside this revetment. The sandbags then support the revetment.

The question of loopholes, drainage, latrines, is dealt with later.

4. *Breastworks.*—Breastworks afford very good cover, but their construction involves much time and very heavy labour. They are therefore usually made only when the state of the ground compels it.

Breastworks are more conspicuous than trenches, but earth breastworks, if well built, do not suffer more heavily than a trench under artillery fire, and are more easily repaired, whilst being very much more comfortable to live in.

Earth breastworks must be at least 10 feet thick at top, and have a very gentle exterior slope. The ditch excavation can be used as an obstacle, and can be filled with wire. When constructing a breastwork one of the most important points to look to is that the near edge of the borrow pit in front of the parapet is far enough from the foot of the interior slope. There is a tendency on the part of the diggers to save themselves labour by digging in towards the parapet. This must be guarded against by marking with a tape a line beyond which there must be no digging, and by constant supervision to see that it is observed. To ascertain the position of this line, find by drawing the minimum width of base necessary to secure a thickness of 10 feet at top, and add at least 2 feet to provide for a berm at the foot of the exterior slope. It will save much time if wooden stretchers are made to carry the earth, and plank gangways are made for the carriers. If no planks or brushwood are available, wire netting laid on the ground will serve to provide a pathway. Work once begun on a breastwork must be completed as quickly as possible, because a new work is likely to prove a tempting target for artillery fire, to which in the early stages it is very vulnerable, and also because it is important to get the work through if possible in the dry. In the kind of site which demands a breastwork, the borrow pit very easily fills with water, and under this condition work becomes very slow and arduous, and may even become impossible. The interior slopes of parapet and parados must be strongly revetted ; hurdlework or some substitute, firmly anchored, forms the best form of revetment ; sandbags do not stand the weather so well. Once the revetment has been put up, digging close to the foot of it must on no account be allowed.

The best method of constructing a breastwork is as follows :— Put up two revetments of gabions or hurdles—or if using sandbags build two sandbag walls—10 feet apart ; fill in between with earth ; build up a bursting course in front ; finally make a very gentle slope to the front.

Breastworks constructed wholly or mainly of sandbags are much more vulnerable to artillery fire than earth breastworks, and are expensive of material. They are to be avoided except for minor works, such as blocking a trench leading towards the enemy, barricading a road, &c. They are, however, often found in the front line, when breastworks have had to be constructed in the presence of the enemy, because they can be made more silently.* They are either formed by gradually raising the parapet of a trench that has become waterlogged, or they may be made by a process of sapping to join up two existing trenches or breastworks. The great fault usually in making these breastworks is to make their sides too straight and steep. The base of such a breastwork must be broader than the top or the whole wall of sandbags will collapse in wet weather.

Breastworks must be constructed with traverses in the same manner as fire trenches, and must have a firing step, to allow of every man using his rifle over the top. The necessary amount of cover for free movement along the line, 6 feet 6 inches as a minimum, can be obtained either by building up the parapet to this height, when a raised firing step will be required, or by having the firing step at ground level and digging a narrow shallow trench immediately behind it and round the ends of traverses. A parados must be constructed to protect the garrison from the back-blast of high explosive shell which burst behind the line. This parados should be about 2 feet 6 inches to 3 feet thick at its base, strongly revetted on both faces. It should be as high or slightly higher than the parapet and as close to it as is compatible with free movement along the line. A path paved with brick or with floor-board gratings just behind the parados is a great convenience; it should communicate with the fire bays by openings through the parados behind at least every other traverse. The space between the breastwork and parados should be floored, and steps taken to allow for drainage from that space.

In a breastwork line, filled sandbags should be stacked close behind the parados at frequent intervals, to be available for

---

* In building parapets, breastworks or revetments with sandbags, the following rules must always be observed:—
  (a) Sandbags should be filled only ¾ full and well beaten into the shape of a brick;
  (b) Sandbags must not be built vertically on one another. A slope of 3/1 is advisable;
  (c) Breaking joint and the use of frequent headers are necessary;
  (d) Each layer of sandbags must be at right angles to the face of the parapet, not horizontal:—

  (e) Sandbags should not be filled with brick rubble; it is dangerous owing to the interstices left between lumps of brick.

25

building up a gap formed by artillery fire, as a speedy temporary repair.

5. *Loopholes.*—All firing by night, and to meet an attack whether by day or by night, must be over the top of the parapet. In all fire trenches, however, a certain number of loopholes are necessary for the use of snipers to inflict casualties on the enemy whenever opportunity offers, to annoy him, interfere with his work, keep him under cover, and keep down the fire of his snipers. Usually one or two loopholes are made in each bay of the fire trenches.

Various types of loophole have been designed, and are in use. It is not intended to describe them in this pamphlet,* but only to lay down the conditions that a satisfactory loophole must fulfil. The most important of these is concealment from the front; for this reason, and to obtain if possible enfilade fire, loopholes should be placed obliquely in the parapet. The maximum amount of cover should be provided for the firer, and the steel loophole plates with a metal flap to close the loophole make probably the best form of loophole. Loopholes should have a curtain (sandbag or some form of cloth) hung on the firer's side, to be used in the same way as a photographer uses a black cloth.

Observing stations and look-out posts behind the lines should be provided with inconspicuous loopholes, but loopholes are not, as a rule, much used for looking out from the trench, except where special loopholes for observation with telescopes are made. Periscopes and small pieces of mirror set up at an angle on the parados give a better view with less exposure.

Loopholes have usually to be made in a parapet at night. The alignment must be carefully sited and marked by day.

6. *Overhead Cover.*—Overhead cover is never used in any trench which is to be occupied as a fire trench. Overhead cover for shelters and dug-outs is dealt with in the paragraph on that subject. Beyond this the only case in which overhead protection is likely to be required is, in rare instances, over very exposed lengths of communication trench and in the form of traverse known as a " bridge " traverse.

7. *Support Trenches.*—Support trenches should be designed as traversed fire trenches, but the supervision trench is usually omitted. Protection against shell fire in the form of deep dug-outs can be made in the support line behind the parados, whereas their use in the front trench interferes with the rapid manning of the trench and is inadmissible. The support line should be connected by numerous communication trenches to the front line, and if there is an obstacle in front of the support line it must be so arranged as not to interfere with the rapid reinforcement of the front line trenches.

8. *Communication Trenches.*—To afford protection from enfilade

---

* Descriptions of various types of loophole will be found in notes that are circulated among the troops from time to time.

fire and to minimise exposure to shrapnel in them, communication trenches must be well bent or traversed. The best type is the winding one, but the curves must be sufficiently pronounced to give real protection against enfilade fire. If traverses are made, the best pattern is an island traverse with the trench going round it on both sides. The corners of traverses should be rounded and not square, as they are easier to pass for a man with a load or for a stretcher,* and are easier to revet. The necessary protection can also be obtained by making the trenches zig-zagged in plan, and this makes revetting easier.

Except in such soil as solid chalk, communication trenches which are required to remain serviceable for a long time or to stand wet weather must be revetted. Experience in Flanders has shown that even if the sides are given as flat a slope as 1/1 they will fall in. A berm of 18 inches should be left between the edge of the trench and the parapet. The minimum width at the bottom should be 2 feet 6 inches, and 3 feet is better. Increasing the width reduces the protection afforded, and the width of 3 feet at the bottom should seldom be exceeded. The revetted sides must be given a slope from 4/1 to 3/1, not cut nearly vertical. The depth of the trench from top of parapet to bottom of trench or floorboard should be 7 feet, if possible; what proportion of this depth is trench and what parapet depends on the site and facilities for drainage. The question of drainage must always receive particular attention in the siting and construction of communication trenches, and they should be boarded, with a drain under the boards, as soon as possible after construction. Passing places and, in a long trench, occasional sidings should be arranged, and signposts should always be placed at the entrance to communication trenches, and at any branches off them, to show where they lead.

Special arrangements must be made to afford protection against the enemy's bombers working down a communication trench to attack one of the lines behind. For this purpose the enemy's bombers must be kept at a distance of not less than 40 yards from the trench to be protected. This can be done by making the last 40 yards of any communication trench, entering a support or cover or back-line trench from the front, straight and providing for machine gun or rifle fire down the straight portion (see fig. 11). A dog-leg trench will do if proper arrangements can be made for enfilading both reaches of it (see fig. 12). Provision must be made for blocking this last 40 yards of the trench at both ends. *Chevaux de frise* ("knife rests") or other wire obstacles, placed in a recess at the point where the block is to be made, so that the last man to retire can quickly pull them down into position as he passes, will do as a temporary expedient for this purpose (see fig. 11).

---

* The minimum curve in winding communication trenches, so that a stretcher can be carried round it by bearers, is 16 foot radius in a trench 3 feet wide.

Communication trenches, if prepared for use as fire trenches, are frequently of the utmost value for flank defence, when the enemy has succeeded in penetrating the front line. The best way of preparing a communication trench for fire is to dig T-heads off the trench so as to form fire bays facing in the required direction, or to cut fire trenches across a re-entrant angle in the trench (see fig. 10) A communication trench prepared for use as a fire trench should be protected on both sides by a good wire entanglement.

18. *Obstacles.**

Front trenches and all trenches which may have to be occupied as fire trenches must be protected by an efficient obstacle. Some form of barbed wire entanglement is the most efficient obstacle and is that universally used. A wire entanglement must be broad enough not to be easily bridged or quickly cut through, must be under the close fire of the defence, and near enough to be effectively watched by night. The near edge of the entanglement should be about 20 yards from the trench, and it should be at least 10 yards broad. A height of 2 feet 6 inches is sufficient, a greater height only increases its liability to damage by our own fire. Every effort must be made to conceal and protect the entanglement; this is best done by sinking it in hollows or trenches. Where trenches are made they should be. of the form shown in fig. 13, *i.e.*, sloping with the maximum depth furthest from the fire trench, so as to minimise the cover which they might afford to the enemy; further, wire sunk in this manner should be carefully sited so that every portion of it is. enfiladed from some point or another in the fire trench. Sunk wire is less visible, less vulnerable to artillery, and less liable to damage by our own fire.

When entanglements are at some distance from the enemy, it may sometimes be useful to construct a second belt of wire beyond the first, with its outer edge some 40 or 50 yards from the trench, to keep hostile bombers at a distance.

Good strong wire entanglements, of the pattern' in fig. 14, fixed to well-driven posts, should be constructed wherever it is possible. With proper training, infantry should be able to make entanglements of this nature as close as 100 yards from the enemy on a dark night. The iron posts now issued, which screw into the ground, can be placed in position without noise and strengthen the entanglement. Only when the opposing lines are too close, or as a temporary means of providing some sort of obstacle quickly, recourse may be had to portable obstacles. The best of these is that known as the "knife rest" (see fig. 15, which sufficiently explains their construction). Two or three rows of these knife rests, placed to break joint and wired together, form a fair obstacle which can be quickly and quietly placed in position. Hollow barbed wire spheres are easily made up in the front trench and

---

* See also Appendix B.

thrown out, and, if plentifully used, are better than no obstacle at all.

The maintenance of the wire obstacle calls for constant care. It must be inspected every night, and a few men should be told off in each company as a permanent wiring party for the repair and improvement of the obstacle.

19. *Protection from Shell Fire.*

1. Protection against loss by shell fire is afforded by details in the design of the trenches themselves, already referred to, *e.g.*, traverses, and keeping trenches as narrow as possible, and is supplemented by the provision of shelters or dug-outs. Shelters may be classified as bomb-proof or splinter-proof, according as they are designed to afford protection against shells hitting them direct and bursting on impact, or against the splinters of shells burst over or near them. It is important to distinguish between the two.

2. The first instinct of the men is to improve the protection afforded by the trench by burrowing out for themselves hollows in the front face, under the parapet ("undercutting"). This practice must be absolutely prohibited. Unless these hollows are very carefully shored up they always result, sooner or later, in the parapet falling in, and, even if the shoring up is efficiently done, the existence of these shelters under the parapet weakens its resistance to the burst of a high-explosive shell.

3. Bomb-proof shelters to ensure protection against heavy high-explosive shells have to be dug deep and entered by a narrow opening and steps. This means that it takes an appreciable time to get men out of them, and as in a well-planned attack the assault will be sudden and unexpected, and the fire of the artillery will not be lifted from the front trench until the leading infantry of the assaulting line is almost into it, they are usually inadmissible in the front line, except for the protection of machine guns and their detachments, and for company headquarters. Deep dug-outs are, moreover, dangerous in an attack by gas.

A certain amount of splinter-proof cover should be provided in the front line, which will also serve as protection against weather. The best position, in the case of a trench, is in the front face of the supervision trench.

4. In the case of strongly constructed breastworks, dug-outs giving good protection against even direct hits by the lighter natures of high-explosive shell can be made under the parapet, and are not so open to the objections which apply to dug-outs in a front fire trench. The parapet over the dug-out must be supported by well-made strong frames and props (see fig. 16).

5. Splinter-proof cover can also be placed behind the parados. In this case protection against back-blast of shells bursting beyond the parados must not be overlooked.

6. No dug-outs must ever be allowed in a trench which interfere with the use of the rifle or free passage along the trench.

7. The use of shelters proof against heavy high-explosive shell in the first system of trenches should therefore generally be confined to the position of the battalion reserves and to "strong points" or "keeps," which may form part of the front system. It is not intended to prohibit their use elsewhere, if the soil or natural features are favourable to their construction, and arrangements can be made to get men out of them quickly, but to point out the dangers that attend their use.

8. Very good protection from a hostile bombardment is afforded by "slit" trenches. These are trenches 1 foot to 2 feet wide and 7 feet deep, dug at right angles to and on either side of the communication trenches. They must be strutted at the top, or they will easily collapse. Each "slit" should be long enough to hold 10 to 12 men (see fig. 3). When they are in use an N.C.O. should be at the end nearest the communication trench. Control is easier when men are sheltered in these "slits" than when in dug-outs. Similar provision can be made further back along the communication trenches for cover for reserves brought up to support a counter-attack.

9. A few notes on the construction of dug-outs are appended. For the construction of deep bomb-proof dug-outs, R.E. advice and assistance will usually be available.

(a) Every deep dug-out must have two or more separate exits to facilitate rapid egress and in case one gets blocked.

(b) Roof timbers must always be made three or four times stronger than is necessary to support merely the load due to the thickness of roof for which they are designed. This is necessary to allow, not only for the shock of the burst of a shell, but also for the possibility that a fresh garrison may take it into their heads to put another 2 or 3 feet of earth on top of the existing roof.

(c) A rectangular timber will support more weight if it stood on its edge, *i.e.*, resting on its shorter side, than when lying flat on its longer side.

(d) The ends of roof timbers should never be supported on sandbag walls or even direct on solid ground. A strong timber frame should always be used on two opposite sides of the shelter to support the ends of roof timbers (see fig. 16).

(e) A "burster" layer, of 6 inches to 1 foot of brick or stone, should always be provided near the top surface of the roof. Over this "burster" layer should be a layer of not less than 6 inches of earth to decrease danger from the scattering of the stone or brick by the burst of the shell. As the object of the "burster" is to explode the shell near the surface, it will be to a large extent defeated if the layer of earth above it is made more than 12 inches thick.

(*f*) Arrangements must be made for ventilating dug-outs. It may occasionally be possible to combine the ventilating pipe with a periscope for look-out purposes.

(*g*) Splinter-proof cover is afforded by a layer of logs or beams, 6 inches or upwards in depth, covered over with a layer of not less than 1 foot of earth. The following forms a roof proof against a 6-inch high explosive shell : A layer of rails or beams, 18 inches of earth, a layer of brick, 2½ feet of earth, another layer of brick 6 inches to 1 foot thick, and over all, 6 inches of earth. The rails or beams must have a good margin of strength over that necessary to support the load above them, so as to stand the shock of the explosion. It will be seen that this roof is fully 6 feet thick. Hence the dug-out will require to be at least 10 feet deep if its position is not to be made too conspicuous.

Fig. 17 shows a typical concreted dug-out.

20. *Machine Gun Emplacements.* (See figs. 18 to 22.)

In view of the great value of machine guns to the defence the siting and construction of emplacements for them requires very special attention and care. Machine guns should be so sited in each line that there is no part of the ground in front of it which is not under their fire. They should be arranged so as to bring a cross fire to bear in front of the trenches which they protect. In this way their power is more fully developed and also concealment is easier. It is important that machine gun emplacements should be constructed so as to be as inconspicuous as possible. Both sides are constantly on the look-out to try and locate the enemy's machine gun emplacements, and any suspected spot is certain, sooner or later, to be made the target for bombardment. For this reason, too, and also to protect them from damage by a chance shell in a general bombardment of the line, emplacements should be made as strong as possible. The ideal arrangement is that each gun should be in a bomb-proof shelter, with overhead cover, and in advance of and to a flank of the part of the line it is to cover. Machine guns in an enclosed emplacement may either be mounted for fire on a fixed line, or so as to have a certain amount of traverse. In the latter case some form of improvised platform mounting, allowing of the gun traversing about its muzzle and not about its centre, enables the size of the loophole to be kept down to a minimum, and is, for this reason, valuable. Machine gun loopholes, at any rate those for use by day, should be as low down in the parapet as possible. Several alternative emplacements should be prepared, some of which may be for using the gun over the top of the parapet. In particular there should be an alternative emplacement, for firing over the top, in connection with each enclosed emplacement and situated close to it. In connection with each of the covered machine gun emplacements there should be provided a good bomb-proof shelter, preferably of the deep dug-out type, to which the crew can temporarily withdraw during a bombardment. This dug-out should communicate direct with the emplacement.

Concrete emplacements can generally be constructed in the reserve trenches.

21. *Latrines.*

The health of the troops demands very careful sanitary arrangements and scrupulous cleanliness in trenches, which may have to be occupied for a considerable length of time. Latrine accommodation must be ample and easy of access; seats should be provided on the scale of at least 2 per cent. of the troops using them. Urine tins should be provided on the same scale. The best place for latrines and urinals for the front line is behind the supervision trench in T-heads at the end of short branches off it. Latrines must be provided for all trenches and shelters which have to be occupied, even for short periods, by troops. The most sanitary system of latrines in trenches is the bucket system, buckets being removed and emptied at night.

A supply of chlorate of lime should be kept in all trenches.

22. *Drainage and Flooring.*

Drainage and precautions for keeping trenches dry and clean, whether they are fire, living, or communication trenches, are questions of great importance, not only from the point of view of preserving the trenches, but also for the health of the troops.

In the case of lines dug deliberately, not in the presence of the enemy, the question of drainage can be carefully studied, and it will often pay to dig drainage trenches of ample capacity before any work on trenches is commenced. Labour spent in this way will be more than repaid. In any case work on drains should keep pace with the progress of the trenches, as trouble is sure to occur if water is allowed to accumulate. For the same reason, care must be taken that the work on each section of trenches is left at an even depth each day when work ceases. Drains should be given a good fall. It will usually pay to revet the sides of an open ditch drain. A good pattern of drain is the box drain, a rectangular channel lined and covered over with planking, laid in the bottom of a trench, which is then covered in again.

In the case of trenches dug in the presence of the enemy the above methods cannot be applied. Drainage is a very difficult problem in these circumstances, even when the ground is not practically flat. Trenches on a forward slope cannot be drained except to the front, and it will seldom be practicable to dig drains leading forward from the trench. Practically all that remains possible as a means of getting rid of the water and keeping trenches reasonably dry and clean is constant pumping and putting down some sort of paving or flooring. Sump-pits, *i.e.*, good deep holes, should be made at intervals to one side of the trench.

They should be revetted and strutted and bridged over with plank covers. From these the water should be pumped out as often as may be necessary over the parapet or the parados, according to which way the ground slopes. If the ground falls to the rear, channels can be cut to lead off into the natural drains of the country and the water pumped into these channels. A channel along the side of the trench or down the centre of it should lead the water into the sump-pits, and it must be constantly cleared. If the channel is cut down the centre of the trench it can be bridged over by special flooring boards, which must be frequently taken up and cleaned. If the level of the water in the ground rises above the level of the floor of the trench, obviously no amount of pumping or digging of sump-pits will keep the trench dry. The only remedy then is to raise the floor of the trench by planks supported on short pile-trestles, and then to raise the parapet accordingly. A most important point is to get some kind of flooring or paving down as soon as possible in any new trench. If this can be done before the mud has been churned up, a great deal of trouble and discomfort will be saved. Floor gratings about 6 feet long and 18 inches to 2 feet wide, made of cross pieces of $\frac{3}{4}$-inch by 4-inch plank, nailed to two longitudinal pieces of timber about 4 inches by 3 inches, on edge, are easily made up, and are a very good form of flooring for trenches.

23. *Defence of Buildings.*

It will often happen that it is considered advisable to include substantial buildings in the front line. Experience has proved that it is extremely hard to dislodge a determined defender from a properly organized building. On the other hand, buildings in or near the front line invariably draw a great deal of artillery fire. For this reason, a building should not normally be occupied by day, unless it either has cellars which can be improved to provide good bomb-proof cover, or similar cover can be made quite close to the house, and connected with it by communication trenches. Otherwise, if the building has been put into a state of defence, a garrison should be detailed who will only occupy it at the last moment in case of attack. A building is strongest for defence when it has been knocked about a bit. The defensive arrangements should be concentrated on the ground floor and cellars; time spent on work on upper stories is sure to be wasted. In the building itself the work to be done is:—

(a) Reinforce the cellar roof, if possible, with concrete; it must be well shored up to enable it to carry the extra protection, and also the *débris* which subsequent shelling will bring down on it.

(b) Loophole the walls for rifle or machine gun fire; the nearer the loopholes are to the ground the better the protection afforded; but there is a risk of falling *débris* blocking them up.

(c) Thicken walls up to the height of the loopholes. This thickening may be done by throwing earth up against the outside of the building, or making a wall of gabions filled with earth or of earth between hurdles, 3 feet clear of the wall of the building, to serve as a burster, but building up inside with brick rubble or earth in sandbags is better, as loopholes near ground level and cellar windows for machine guns can then be used.

(d) Block up and loophole ground floor windows and doors.

(e) Erect overhead cover over fire positions. This should be in the form of a false roof, preferably of concrete, otherwise of heavy rails or very stout timbers carried on very substantial timber supports, or on rails or girders. This roof will protect the firers from falling *débris*, and the more the house is knocked about the stronger will the cover become.

(f) Improve internal communications by gapping internal walls where necessary.

In connection with the defence of the building there may also be fire trenches in front of it and to either flank communicating by trenches with one another and with the building, the whole forming practically a small strong point of which the house is the keep. "Slit trenches, such as have already been described, situated close behind the house and connected with it by a communication trench, form a useful adjunct to the defensive arrangements.

24. *Training in Digging, &c.*

Infantry must be capable of the construction, repair, and maintenance, without R.E. assistance, of all forms of trenches, shelters (except deep bomb-proof dug-outs), and barbed wire entanglements. Constant practice in digging and making entanglements at night is necessary. Officers and men must be well trained in the method of marking out works to be dug at night and in extending a party silently on a task in darkness. Troops should be trained to dig, &c., fully equipped (except for their packs).

It will be found useful to have a certain number of men in each company specially trained under R.E. supervision in the construction of barbed-wire entanglements, loopholes, revetting, drainage, &c.

CHAPTER III.

OCCUPATION AND RELIEF OF TRENCHES AND GENERAL TRENCH ROUTINE.

25. *System of Relief of Trenches.*

It is absolutely essential that in every unit a thoroughly sound system of carrying out reliefs is established. If the proper arrangements are made and the necessary precautions observed, the relief of trenches can be accomplished, with a little experience, safely and expeditiously. Carelessly conducted reliefs, on the other hand, involve not only great and unnecessary danger to the security of the trench line but avoidable loss of life and discomfort to the men.

The first essential is a careful preliminary reconnaissance. Whenever a unit is about to take over a new line of trenches, parties from it will visit the trenches previously, by day if possible. In the case of a battalion, the party should consist of the C.O., adjutant and machine gun officer, and at least one officer and one N.C.O. from each company. It will often be advisable, especially when taking over a new line and in the case of inexperienced troops, that one officer and N.C.O. from each company should remain a complete 24 hours in the trenches previous to the arrival of the battalion. The snipers of the relieving unit should be in the trenches for 24 hours before the relief takes place.

Detailed information from the unit to be relieved must be obtained on the following points :—*

(a) Condition of wire entanglement, parapet, &c.
(b) Work in progress.
(c) Position of hostile machine guns, snipers, &c., as far as known.
(d) Danger points, *e.g.*, where saps run out, portions of trench especially subject to enfilade fire, &c.
(e) Position of listening posts.
(f) Position of S.A.A. reserve, bomb stores and trench stores.
(g) List of trench stores.†
(h) Method of communication with supporting artillery.

---

* A Trench "Log Book" kept up daily by each unit in the trenches and handed over to the relieving unit, is a convenient method of recording changes in the trench line and all other information of value regarding the trenches. Such a record is of great assistance to ensure continuity of work.

† Trench stores are the articles which remain permanently in the trenches and are handed over from one unit to another. They include S.A.A., grenades, tools, pumps, loophole plates, braziers, &c.

(*i*) Arrangements: if heavily shelled; to meet an attack; for counter-attack.
(*j*) Any arrangements for visual signalling or communication by rockets.
(*k*) Sanitary arrangements.
(*l*) Water supply.
(*m*) Arrangements for cooking and supplying hot meals.
(*n*) Route by which first line transport brings up rations at night and where rations are dumped.

A map of the trench line should also be obtained.

26. *Description of Method of Carrying out a Relief.*

1. The following summary of the steps to be taken in the case of the relief of one brigade by another in the trench line is given as a guide to the normal procedure :—

(*a*) On receiving orders to take over some portion of the line, the Brigade Staff obtain from the brigade to be relieved all available information regarding the line, work in progress, ammunition and stores available, &c., make what reconnaissance of the line the Brigadier considers necessary, and arrange with the other brigade the details of the relief. It is important that the O.C. Brigade Machine Gun Company should make a thorough reconnaissance of the line.

(*b*) When the Brigade Staff have arranged how the line is to be held they make the necessary arrangements to enable battalions to carry out their reconnaissance of the line as detailed in Section 25.

It must be remembered that units of an ingoing brigade may not be of the same strength as the units to be relieved. A battalion may not, therefore, take over exactly the same frontage as is held by a battalion in the line, but may take over trenches from two battalions. This case necessitates careful arrangements as regards guides and the handing and taking over.

(*c*) Reliefs, except in very favourable circumstances, have usually to be carried out under cover of darkness. The time of commencement of relief will depend on local circumstances and conditions, but it is generally advisable to begin reliefs as early as possible. In order to prevent the enemy from detecting our system of reliefs the intervals between reliefs and the hours at which they are carried out should be varied from time to time.

2. The brigade marches off from its billets by battalions, with an interval of about half an hour between battalions on the same road.* Transport accompanying units must be kept down to a minimum and a point must be fixed beyond which it is not allowed to proceed. It is usually at this point that guides from the unit

---

* If relief takes place by day, at least two hours interval must be left between times of starting for different battalions. Relieving battalions then move up by platoons to the meeting place for guides.

to be relieved meet the battalions. Any stores, &c., to be carried up to the trenches,* which may so far have been carried for convenience on the transport, are distributed amongst the men at this point, and the relief then usually proceeds by companies or smaller parties, each with its set of guides provided by the unit to be relieved.

It is usual to provide a guide from each platoon as well as guides for battalion headquarters, and for machine guns. Every guide must be in the possession of a paper showing the number or name of his trench, and the number of men in it.

3. The following notes on equipment for the trenches may be useful:—

Packs are taken to the trenches, except in the case of units going to the trenches to make an attack. Men take waterproof ground sheets, but blankets should not be taken. Every man should carry two sandbags tucked into his belt.

All officers should have electric torches, and a long pole is very useful. Waterproof waders or overalls to the knee are very useful in wet weather.

27. *Precautions and Arrangements necessary during a Relief.*

The following are notes on some of the points to be observed in carrying out reliefs. It is advisable to embody some instructions on these points in Standing Orders for Trench Warfare.

(*a*) All units should be formed up before dark in the order in which and under the commander with whom they will go into the trenches.

(*b*) All parties must be kept closed up while moving to and from the trenches; the pace in front must be *very* slow. An officer should always be in rear. On dark nights it is often advisable for each man of a party to hold the bayonet scabbard of the man in front. Nothing causes confusion, unnecessary fatigue, and loss of moral so much as men getting lost from their parties while moving up to the trenches.

(*c*) Reliefs will be carried out as quietly as possible; no lights or smoking are allowed after reaching a point to be decided on by the battalion commander.

(*d*) Before commencing a relief every party must receive orders as to what action is to be taken by them in the event of an attack or alarm taking place while reliefs are in progress. Any retirement of troops should be avoided on principle. As a general rule, parties caught in the open during a relief should occupy the nearest trench or cover available and get into touch at once with the nearest body of troops holding the trench line.

As far as circumstances permit, and especially whenever there is a probability of attack, reliefs should be carried out gradually, so that too many men are not moving in the open at the same time.

---

* Rations for 48 hours and 150 rounds S.A.A. are usually carried on the man, when going into the trenches.

(e) No trench or post should ever be evacuated by the troops to be relieved until the relieving troops have actually occupied it. The method of carrying out the actual relief of a trench must vary according to the nature of the trenches. The following is a usual method :—

The platoon being relieved gets on the firing step. The relieving platoon files in behind and halts. On the word "Pass," which will be given quietly, being passed along, the relieved and relieving platoons change places. The new sentries, who will have been told off prior to the new platoon coming into the trenches, will take over from the old sentries, and the relieved platoon will file out. Where the trenches are too narrow to permit of above, the relieving troops must lie down behind the parados of the fire trench whilst the relief of sentries is carried out. Before dismissing the relieving platoon, the platoon commander will satisfy himself that all sentries have been properly posted and that every man can aim at the bottom of his own wire from the position allotted him.

(f) On taking over any trench the officer in charge will obtain all the information available, will take over the stores and tools in the trench, have the men told off in sentry groups and the first reliefs posted. He will ascertain at once the position of the trenches on his flanks and of the nearest supports, sending out patrols to get into touch with them and act as guides. He will ensure that he has a sufficient number of guides who know the way to company and battalion headquarters.

(g) The completion of a relief must be reported at once—by the company commander to battalion headquarters when the relief of the company is complete, by the battalion commander to brigade headquarters when the relief of the battalion is complete, and by brigade headquarters to divisional headquarters when the relief of the brigade is complete. Both relieved and relieving units must make these reports. The battalion and brigade staffs of units relieved must remain till the relief of all the troops under them has been completed.

28. *Handing over Trenches.*

Officers handing over trenches are responsible that all available information and trench maps of the locality are given to the relieving unit, and that all tools and trench stores are collected and handed over in the most convenient way and place.

A supply of Very lights and other consumable stores sufficient for at least 24 hours should be handed over to the relieving unit.

Lists of stores and reports on trenches, giving all available information, must, whenever possible, be prepared and handed over to relieving units on the day previous to relief taking place.

29. *Duties in Trenches.*

The following precautions for the safety of the trench line must invariably be observed :—

(a) By night, at least one man in every four, and by day at least one in every ten, will be on the look-out in each trench.*

(b) All men in the fire trench, and a proportion of men in the support trench, will always wear their equipment (except packs). Equipment may be taken off by order of a company commander in the case of working parties, when it will be kept close at hand. Every man will be told off to a particular post in case of attack; he will not leave the proximity of his post without the permission of his immediate commander, nor leave the trench without the permission of an officer. Bayonets will always be fixed in the fire trench during the hours of darkness, during a snow storm or thick mist, or whenever the proximity of the enemy renders this course advisable.

All sentries are posted and relieved by a N.C.O. told off by each platoon for that purpose. One officer per company should be always on duty, and these N.C.Os. report to him hourly. The officer on duty should be continually moving up and down to see that all is correct.

(c) Where enemy's lines are more than 100 or 150 yards away, a listening post should be established by each platoon, in a sap communicating with the front trench, and at a distance of approximately one-third of the distance to enemy's trench. These posts usually consist of three men and one N.C.O., and are posted at dusk and relieved every four hours. *All* the men of the post are awake for the four hours they are on duty. The officer on duty should visit listening posts twice each night.

(d) Machine guns will be in position and ready loaded by night, by day they may for purposes of concealment be removed, provided they can be immediately placed in position in the event of an attack; one man must always be on the look-out at each machine gun, and the detachment must remain in close proximity to their gun.

(e) In every trench some form of alarm must be arranged to signal the approach of gas. Whistles should not be used for this purpose. The precautions against attacks by gas are dealt with in special instructions issued to the troops.

(f) Officers in a trench should be divided up along the trench, and must not all be together, especially at night. All the officers of a company must not live in one dug-out, as one shell might knock them all out.

Attacks prepared by artillery fire are most usually made at dawn, as soon as it is light enough for the artillery to observe, or about one hour before dusk. The former is usually the case in attacks on a large scale, or when a prolonged artillery bombardment precedes the attack, the latter when an attack on a small

---

* A good system is to work in groups of six men under a N.C.O. By night, two men of each group are on sentry. By day, only one man of each group is on sentry and the number of groups may be reduced. The number of groups must depend on proximity of enemy's trenches, nature of ground, &c.

scale is to be prepared and carried out before dusk, and the position won then consolidated under cover of darkness.

Units (including reserves) should stand to arms about one hour before dawn and before dusk.

30. *Usual Routine in Trenches.*

1. Rifles must be inspected twice daily, morning and evening, and every precaution must be taken to keep them and all other equipment in good order.* Men should be required to produce their oil bottles at rifle inspection.

2. The chief problem to be faced in the ordinary routine of trench work is to ensure that the maximum amount of work is done daily towards the subjection and annoyance of the enemy and the improvement of the trenches, consistent with the necessity for every man to get a proper amount of rest and sleep. This can only be done by a good system, a definite programme and time table of work being arranged and adhered to as far as possible. Some notes on the system of work in trenches are given in the next section:

3. Rations for 48 hours should be taken into the trenches on the man whenever possible, in order to save the labour of bringing up and distributing rations to the trenches every night. A quantity of sandbags and other stores and material have usually to be carried up to the trenches every night, and the arrangements for carrying parties require careful organization and forethought. The principle to be followed is that parties are detailed from behind to carry up rations or stores to troops in front, so as to avoid troops in front line having to send back parties and thus weaken their line. Thus the battalion reserve supplies carrying parties up to the front line trenches, and the brigade reserve may have to find carrying parties up to the battalion reserve or to the front trenches. Usually it will be possible to bring stores as far as the battalion reserve on pack animals or improvised handcarts. Ration parties and carrying parties must always be armed, wearing the rifle slung.

4. The system by which a unit in the trenches obtains the material required for the construction and repair of the trenches is as follows. In every brigade a "brigade workshop" is usually formed, the necessary personnel (from 12 to 20 men) being found from men in the battalions who are carpenters and artificers by trade. The "brigade workshop" is administered by the Staff Captain of the brigade, with a reliable N.C.O. in charge. It is established as near the trench line as possible, consistent with the men being able to

---

* Every care must be taken to prevent loss of equipment, &c., of which a great and usually avoidable waste may occur through lack of supervision, especially by junior officers. All rifles, ammunition (including fired cases), equipment, tools, trench stores, &c., found lying about within the area held by a unit must invariably be collected, at a pre-arranged dumping ground, special parties being detailed by units for this purpose, if necessary. A list of articles so collected by any unit should be sent to Brigade Headquarters, who will issue instructions as to their disposal.

work in reasonable safety. Its functions are to make up the material obtained from the R.E. into shapes and sizes suitable for carrying up to the trenches, to construct any simple device required for use in the trenches, and to carry out the distribution of the material. The brigade workshop makes up, for instance, barbed wire "knife rests," box loopholes, rifle rests, floor gratings, grenade boxes, signboards for communication trenches, &c.

Each unit in the trenches sends in daily to brigade headquarters, as early in the morning as possible, a request for the material required to be brought up that night. The Staff Captain arranges for its preparation in the brigade workshop and for sending it up to battalion headquarters, who arrange for its further distribution to companies.

31. *Work in Trenches.*

1. The importance of working on a definite system and with a definite programme has already been emphasised. The essential requirements for a fire trench are given in Section 17, and must always receive first attention—the barbed wire entanglement must be at least 10 yards wide, and concealed as far as possible.

The following points come next in order of importance :—

(*a*) The provision of good loopholes for snipers, at least one per section of men in the trench.

(*b*) The construction or improvement of communication trenches; there should be one per platoon from the support line to the fire trench, if possible. From the support line to the reserve line, two per battalion will suffice.

(*c*) Listening posts, one per platoon, pushed well forward.

(*d*) The construction of bomb-proof or splinter-proof shelter. (See Section 19.)

(*e*) The provision of S.A.A. and grenade stores should be two S.A.A. reserve stores,* and one grenade store per platoon. Both S.A.A. and grenades should be stored in depth, *i.e.*, a proportion should be stored in the support and reserve lines as well as in the front line. Suitable positions for these stores are at the points where communication trenches run into the various lines.

(*f*) An inspection trench (behind parados) and bombing pits or trenches (see page 22) may be made if required.

2. When sandbags are to be filled for any work in the trenches, they must not be filled by taking earth from holes made indiscriminately in the ground behind the trenches, as this practice makes this ground difficult to walk over and often interferes with the construction of fresh trenches. A trench which will serve some useful purpose should be made when earth for filling sandbags is required. When filled sandbags have to be carried for any distance, it is preferable to have separate parties for filling and carrying.

---

* In addition to the S.A.A. carried by the men (150 rounds), a supply equivalent to 120 rounds per man should be kept in the trenches and a reserve of 10 to 20 boxes at battalion headquarters.

3. It will be found convenient to have in every company a proportion of men specially trained under R.E. supervision in making loopholes, laying out barbed wire, revetting, &c. All men must, of course, be practised in these duties, but a specially trained squad for the more technical work will be found a great assistance.

4. As a rough guide to the number of men available for work in the trenches, it may be assumed that a company in the trenches will number about 160, leaving out signallers, machine gunners, orderlies, &c. Of these there will be by day about 16 to 20 men engaged in observation and sniping, and another 16 to 20 ready to relieve them. This will leave about 120 available for work, and it should be possible to arrange for them to do two hours' work in the morning and two in the afternoon. By night 40 sentries will be required, and the next relief of 40 must not be required to work before going on duty. The number of sentries by night may be reduced, if parties are working out in front of the trench.

5. The above notes are to be taken as a guide only. Local conditions vary the order of importance in which work should be undertaken. In some trenches it is impossible to do much work to the trenches by day.

The infantry must always be prepared to assist any R.E. and miners working in their section of the line.

32. *Observation and Sniping.*

1. A good system of sniping and observation is of the utmost importance in trench warfare. Usually every battalion has a special detachment of trained snipers working under a selected officer or N.C.O. Their duties are to keep the enemy's lines under constant observation, note any changes in the line and any new work undertaken by the enemy, keep the enemy's snipers in check, and to inflict casualties on the enemy whenever opportunity offers.

2. The following are the chief essentials for a successful sniping organization :—

(a) Careful selection and training of snipers ;
(b) Well-chosen and well-concealed posts or loopholes ;
(c) A good system which will ensure all parts of the enemy's line being kept under constant observation ;
(d) Good discipline, which will prevent posts being given away by carelessness ;
(e) Care of equipment ;
(f) Individual ingenuity in using disguises, masks, dummies, and other devices.

3. The following notes on the above points may be found of use :—

(a) *Selection and Training of Snipers.*—Men selected must be intelligent and well educated, besides being good shots. Observation and the ability to describe what he has seen are most important qualifications in a sniper.

The following are the chief points in which he should receive training:—

Shooting at vanishing and moving objects.
Judging distance.
Observation of bullet strike.
Use and care of optical sights.
Use and care of telescopes, field glasses, and periscopes.
Use of natural and construction of artificial cover.
Assimilation of colour to surroundings.
Construction of all types of loopholes and bullet-proof cover.
Value of immobility and silence and necessity of patience.
Map reading.
Writing of simple reports.
Eyesight training.
Location by means of flash and sound of hostile riflemen.

Snipers should be kept well informed; they should be shown aeroplane photographs of the enemy's position, and any information of interest to them from intelligence reports, examination of captured prisoners, &c., should be passed to them.

(b) *Choice and Concealment of Positions.*—No definite rules can be laid down as to the best positions for snipers. It must be left to the ingenuity and enterprise of the sniping officer or snipers to discover suitable places and to utilise them skilfully. Many excellent places will be found for observation and sniping in rear of the firing line. The best time to reconnoitre for such points is during the evening light, when the enemy cannot see any distance, but while it is still possible to see whether they command the view required.

The building of loopholes so as to make them secure, invisible, and convenient for observing and firing at definite points is an art in itself and gives endless openings for originality. Loopholes usually have to be let into the parapet by night and this must be practised, as the work has to be done quickly so as to be completed by daylight. The concealment of loopholes is made much easier if the outer face of the parapet is irregular. The Germans in many places take great pains to give an irregular outline to their parapet, using beams, timber, bolsters, mattresses and all sorts of rubbish piled up against it. A tunnel through the parapet, if the opening is carefully concealed, may form a good sniper's post.

The use of veils and coats of a colour to match the background is useful. If near sandbags, an empty sandbag worn over the head is a good disguise. Against an earth background a brown gauze veil, against grass a green one are both difficult to detect. Grass, weeds, wood or branches may give concealment.

Dummy loopholes are of great value to attract enemy's fire.

(c) *System.*—Posts should be so arranged that the whole front of the enemy's line opposite the battalion sector is under observation from dawn till dusk, each post having a definite front to watch. Snipers should work in pairs, one observing while the other is in readiness to shoot. Four men in two reliefs should be told off to each post.

Each post should be made to render a report daily under the following headings :—

Any new work done by the enemy.

Machine guns, trench mortars, snipers, observation posts, new loopholes, &c., located during the day.

Germans seen, place, uniform, apparent age, physique, equipment.

Any of the enemy fired at, any evidence to show they were hit.

Any other information of interest.

All rifles and optical equipment must be carefully cleaned on coming off duty, and should be inspected daily by an officer.

Snipers should not usually be required to do any night work, the duty of constant observation by day is a trying one, and, with the cleaning and care of the equipment, a sniper's time will be fully occupied.

(d) *Discipline.*—Good discipline is necessary to prevent carelessness in giving away posts by exposure or by wild and unnecessary firing. The battalion snipers are apt to develop into "scallywags" in habit and appearance, unless good discipline is strictly enforced.

(e) *Care of Equipment.*— This has already been mentioned above. It must be remembered that telescopic sights are most delicate instruments and require testing and adjustment by an expert if good results are to be obtained.

4. When a battalion is taking over a new line, the battalion snipers should, whenever possible, spend 24 hours in the new trenches with the snipers of the battalion to be relieved, in order to obtain all the information available from them and to become acquainted with the new line.

5. If a line is taken over in which the enemy's snipers have been allowed to get the upper hand, the first task is the location of the hostile snipers' posts. The enemy's loopholes should be searched for systematically all along the parapets, together with any likely sniping-places in rear. The trees, sandbags, &c., in our own trenches should be searched for rifle bullet marks which may show the direction of the hostile snipers. Sentries should be warned to try and discover from what point sniping is coming, and to watch for any flashes at night. When all possible has been done to locate the enemy's sniping, a system of loopholes should be decided on by which every part of the enemy's line can be observed and fired on from some secure position.

6. Co-operation between neighbouring units is essential. Often the best position to observe and fire on a certain portion of the line is in the sector of the battalion on the flank.

7. Fixed rifle batteries for keeping certain points or localities under fire by night are often extremely useful as a means of hampering the enemy's work and causing loss.

33. *Co-operation with Artillery.*

1. *Arrangements for Intercommunication.*—A certain force of artillery is detailed for the support of each infantry brigade holding a portion of the line. Batteries are allotted to sectors, and the points on which guns are normally layed* are selected by the infantry brigade commander in consultation with the artillery. The zones of fire allotted to adjacent batteries should overlap, if possible, at specially dangerous or important points.

The following system of communication between infantry and artillery has been found to answer well :—

> A code number or letter is given to each place on which guns are layed and a sketch showing the code is kept by the company commander in the trenches, by the battalion commander, at the battery O.P., and the battery. A direct line is laid from the trenches (at some selected company headquarters) to the battery. When fire is required at night on any particular point, it is sufficient to telephone down the code letter or number, and the gun concerned opens fire at once. If fire is required on any other place, it should be described with reference to one of the selected points. If this system is used, careful instructions as to the occasions on which artillery fire may be called for and a good understanding on the point between the infantry and artillery are necessary. Infantry must understand that firing by night is apt to give away the gun positions, so unnecessary requests for fire must be avoided ; on the other hand, frequent opportunities arise of doing the enemy damage by artillery fire at night and can only be taken advantage of if there is close co-operation between the infantry and artillery.
>
> In order not to give away permanent gun positions, it has been found to be a good plan to lay out night lines for single guns from positions to be taken up by night to deal with any special target.

The arrangements for the action of the artillery in case of an attack by the enemy are dealt with in Section 41, Chapter IV.

2. *Aggressive Action.*—In order to obtain full benefit from aggressive artillery action, close co-operation between infantry and artillery is essential. Every means must be used to induce the enemy to man his parapets or come out and expose himself and then to catch him with infantry and artillery fire. Various schemes will suggest themselves, and can be worked out between infantry and artillery commanders.

It is a good thing to have a number of schemes both of retaliation and of aggressive action worked out and communicated to all

---

* Usually known as the " night lines."

concerned, so that they can be put into force at once by a message—" Scheme No. ."

3. *Information.*—The artillery require all the assistance they can get as to location of targets and the effect of their fire. Every endeavour should be made by the infantry to assist, and artillery observing posts should be connected to the front trenches for this purpose.

Infantry officers should be instructed in artillery methods of describing the position of targets, and it is a great advantage both to infantry and artillery if arrangements can be made for every infantry officer in turn to spend a few hours in the artillery observation station overlooking his part of the line. It helps him to know the country from an artillery point of view.

In describing targets, reference should always be made to points in the enemy's line, not to portions of our own line. The same names should therefore be given by infantry and artillery to prominent objects in the enemy's line.

The following rules should always be observed in reports sent by the infantry to the artillery :—

(i) The time and the observer's position must be accurately stated.
(ii) If reporting on enemy's artillery fire it must be stated whether shrapnel or H.E. The direction from which the shells are coming should be given as accurately as possible.

The fuzes of German shells frequently furnish valuable information to the artillery. They should be sent at once to the nearest artillery unit, with a statement as to where they were found.

4. *Artillery Observation Posts.*—Careful instructions are necessary to prevent artillery observation posts being given away by infantry approaching them without precaution. On the other hand artillery have been known to draw fire on infantry positions by approaching headquarters, reserve positions, etc., without concealment.

34. *Sanitation and Care of Feet.*

In view of the length of time during which the same line of trenches frequently has to be occupied, special precaution must be taken to keep trenches in a clean and sanitary state. A latrine system of buckets or tins must be arranged whenever possible. A supply of chlorate of lime will be kept in each trench and used daily. Places for burying all tins and rubbish should be carefully chosen as far from the trench as is practicable and should be marked.

Bodies of dead men will be taken right away from the trenches to be buried.

The disease known as " trench feet " is caused by prolonged standing in cold water or mud and by the continued wearing of wet socks, boots, and puttees. It is brought on much more rapidly when the blood circulation is interfered with by the use of tight boots, tight puttees, or the wearing of anything calculated to cause constriction of the lower limbs. It can be prevented by :—

(a) Improvements to trenches leading to dry standing and warmth.

(b) Regimental arrangements ensuring that the men's feet and legs are well rubbed with whale oil or anti-frostbite grease before entering the trenches, and that, so far as is possible, men reach the trenches with dry boots, socks, trousers, and puttees.*

(c) By taking every opportunity while in the trenches to have boots and socks taken off from time to time, the feet dried, well rubbed, and dry socks (of which each man should carry a pair) put on.

(d) By arrangements to give the men some exercise daily so as to maintain the blood circulation.

(e) By the provision of warm food in the trenches when possible, and by the provision of warmth, shelter, hot food, and facilities for washing the feet and drying wet clothes for men leaving the trenches.

It is important to keep 50 extra pairs of boots in a battalion, so that men whose boots need repair can be given another pair while theirs are being mended. This can be done by battalion or brigade arrangements, a small shoemaker's establishment being kept up, which can go on working while the battalion is in the trenches.

35. *Communications.*

Communications in the trench line are established by telephone, but it must be realised that in the event of heavy shelling all telephonic communication is likely to be interrupted, and an efficient alternative system of visual signalling and a service of orderlies must be arranged and tested.

The Adjutant is responsible for the communications of his battalion. Battalion signals are responsible for all communications from battalion headquarters forward. The Brigade Signal Section is responsible for communications from brigade headquarters to battalion headquarters.

It is the duty of all ranks to assist the Signal Service in the following ways :—

(a) Reporting breaks in lines to the nearest Signal Station.

(b) Taking care to prevent damage to lines by troops or wagons, even if lines are badly laid.

(c) Taking into the nearest Signal section any telephone equipment found lying about.

(d) Preventing any unauthorized persons interfering with lines ; anyone seen interfering with cables who has not a blue and

---

* Long gum boots are issued for use in the trenches and should be put on *while the men's feet are still dry.* Gum boots should not be kept on longer than absolutely necessary, as owing to lack of ventilation, men's feet sweat freely, and the inside of the boot becomes wet.

white armlet should be asked his business and sent to the nearest Headquarters if his answers are not satisfactory ; any civilian seen touching lines should immediately be arrested.

Where telephone lines cross roads or tracks used by troops or communication trenches, &c., they must be buried or put up at such a height as not to impede movement. All telephone lines should be labelled at frequent intervals.

An efficient system of communication by orderlies must be arranged, and long messages, unless urgent, should, whenever possible, be sent by orderly to avoid congestion of telephone lines. Within a brigade, each battalion details two permanent bicycle orderlies, who remain with brigade headquarters for the purpose of taking messages to their battalions. Battalions are responsible that they always have at least two orderlies (in addition to the permanent brigade orderlies) who know the way to brigade headquarters. There must also be at battalion headquarters guides to every trench held by the battalion.

Men should constantly be sent with messages at night so that they may know their way about. They should be able to describe accurately the position of their trench to the persons to whom they take the messages.

Headquarters should never be changed unless absolutely necessary, as it causes dislocation of the signal arrangements. Any unit which changes its headquarters must at once inform the unit above, and send an orderly to it to act as a guide to the new headquarters.

The Signal Service is responsible for giving the correct time, and watches should be set by signal time.

36. *Reports.*

Periodical situation reports are required from units in the trenches at stated hours, usually at morning, noon, and evening. The direction of the wind should be given in situation reports, as this affects the possibility or otherwise of a gas attack by the enemy.

Any unusual occurrence is, of course, reported at once, and any important change of wind should also be reported.

A casualty report and fighting strength return are required daily from units as soon after noon as possible.

A list of material required for the trenches should be rendered as early as possible in the morning (see p. 40).

Staffs must avoid burdening units in the trench line with unnecessary returns and correspondence ; units, on the other hand, must remember that delay or carelessness in rendering reports and returns causes unnecessary work to the staff.

CHAPTER IV.

ORGANIZATION OF A TRENCH LINE AND ACTION IN CASE OF
ATTACK.

37. *General Considerations.*

The importance of organizing a line of trenches, and the distribution of the garrison within it, on a definite scheme and with a definite object, is sufficiently obvious. There is, however, a tendency, due usually to a lack of guidance from above, and also to the frequent changes of units in a line, to lose sight of this and to remain content to make the best of what is found existing. In such circumstances the defensive line becomes a haphazard collection of trenches, and the organization of their defence or of an offensive movement from them is a matter of great difficulty.

The objects to be sought in the organization of a system of trenches are:—

(a) To render the front line invulnerable to any small assaults by the enemy, and to create behind it a defensive zone of such depth as will not only make it impossible for an attack, in whatever strength it is made, to penetrate the whole of our defensive system, but will cause the enemy such loss, and so disorganize his attacking forces, as to enable our reserves to inflict on them a decisive defeat.

(b) To enable an attack on the enemy's defences to be made under the most favourable conditions and with the minimum of warning to the enemy. To this end our front line of trenches should be pushed within assaulting distance of the enemy's front line, and the arrangement of the trenches be such that the attacking troops can be distributed under the best conditions.

(c) In the normal periods of trench warfare, to reduce, by the improvement of the trenches and an economical distribution of the garrison, the wastage in our own forces, both from battle casualties and from disease; and by skilful sniping and constant small enterprises to harass and inflict loss on the enemy.

Local conditions will largely determine the relative importance of the foregoing considerations. In a line of such length as now exists, there will be certain portions in which there are no objectives of sufficient importance to make an attack on a large scale either by ourselves or the enemy probable; on such portions of the front the aim is by good organization of the defence and minor offensive enterprises to compel the enemy to keep as large or a larger garrison than ourselves, and to increase his rate of wastage compared to our own. On other portions of the front there may be some objective which is likely to be the aim of a hostile attack, whereas an advance on our part would result in no commensurate gain ; in such a case the organization of the defence is of paramount importance. Or again, these conditions may be exactly reversed.

On a small scale, the same considerations apply to a brigade or battalion front. Certain features are of tactical importance, while certain lengths of trench offer no particular advantage to either side. Thus the distribution of the garrison and the construction of the defences must be founded on clear tactical ideas and not on a uniform distribution of so many men to so many yards of front.

38. *Distribution of Men in Trenches.*

By day, provided there is a good obstacle in front, covered by the cross-fire of machine guns, and supports can be moved up rapidly, the front line should be held lightly, in order to minimise loss from shell fire and the enemy's snipers, and to enable the majority of the men to obtain better rest and shelter in the support and reserve lines. By night, the front line must be held in sufficient strength to repulse raids by the enemy, and to prevent his reconnoitring patrols from penetrating the front line ; and also because in a line held thinly by night the men are apt to become "jumpy."

The question of the number of men placed in the front line of trenches is, however, to a certain extent, affected by the question of upkeep of the trenches. Experience has shown that trenches cannot be kept from falling in unless continuous work on their repair is carried on. In order, therefore, to keep a line of trenches habitable, it is often necessary to keep constantly in them a sufficient number of men to do the necessary work.

The distribution of a battalion in the trenches will usually consist of two or three companies in the front line finding their own supports and two or one companies in battalion reserve. Battalion headquarters should be close to the position of the battalion reserve, and will be connected by telephone to headquarters of companies.

It has been found by experience that in trench warfare it is advisable to make each company self-contained, *i.e.*, each company should have its own trained grenadiers with a sufficient supply of grenades, its own snipers, and men trained in laying out barbed wire, making loopholes, &c. There may be in addition a party of battalion grenadiers or battalion snipers, specially trained and organized for any special work.

39. *Machine Guns.*

1. *Distribution.*—The extra fire power now placed in the hands of brigade and battalion commanders by the increase in the

number of machine guns enables men to be economized in the front trenches and a larger force thus left available for counter-attack.

A natural tendency is to place every available machine gun in the first line trenches, in order to establish an impassable curtain of fire in front of them. In the case of a bombardment, these trenches are liable to be very badly damaged and most of the machine guns may be destroyed. Any which have been located will certainly be put out of action. This tendency must therefore be suppressed.

The object to be aimed at is to place machine guns in such a way that if, after a bombardment or by the use of asphyxiating gas, the enemy succeeds in penetrating our lines, his infantry, at every step of their advance, will be met with fire from machine guns which have been previously echeloned in depth, and will thus be compelled to stop.

It is not so necessary to cover a large area with fire as to arrange for flanking fire from well selected positions; this fire will sweep away the waves of hostile infantry as they try to push forward.

Commanders must therefore divide their machine guns between the front line and the ground in rear of it, and in each particular case must see that the emplacements blend with the surrounding ground and fit in with the general scheme of defence.

The commander of the brigade machine gun company must always make a careful study of the whole sector held by the brigade, with a view to ensuring that the guns are placed to the best advantage. Co-operation must be arranged on the flanks of the sector with the machine gun companies of the neighbouring brigades.

2. *Protection and Concealment.*—A really bomb-proof emplacement for machine guns requires considerable thickness of cover, and in the open this fact will render it liable to be easily located by the enemy, who will be able to destroy it if he thinks it worth while.

Bomb-proof emplacements must therefore only be placed in positions where the enemy cannot observe them, such as on reverse slopes, or where their relief conforms to the folds of the ground, or in woods, &c.

The importance of keeping machine guns invisible in places where a bomb-proof emplacement cannot be concealed necessitates the firing emplacements being made outside the shelters, but they must be near enough for the guns to be brought into action at a moment's notice. The shelters are only to be used to protect the teams, and can therefore be dug as deep as required and so have an almost invisible relief.

Firing emplacements must be *as near the shelters as possible.* They can either be protected against splinters by light overhead cover, or be in the parapet without any head cover at all.

Firing emplacements can also be prepared in holes in the open in front of or behind the fire trench. These holes should be connected with the shelters by underground passages. The gun should be mounted at the last moment on the extreme edge of the hole, either without any protection at all, or, preferably, masked by a shield or gently sloping parapet. If the hole and its surroundings are carefully disguised, it will certainly escape observation by the enemy. Such emplacements should be frequently used behind the first lines (see fig. 22).

When a fire trench is dug on a reverse slope, a very useful method when the amount of work involved is not prohibitive is to dig such holes in front of the ridge and connect them with the trench by underground passages running under the ridge itself.

Machine guns can also be placed in trees in the same way as observation posts.

In order to ensure invisibility, all communication trenches leading to the emplacements must be constructed as blinded saps. It is also essential to prepare a large number of emplacements in order to avoid firing daily from those which are specially constructed for the purpose of repelling an attack.

Machine gunners must never abandon their position in any circumstances. If necessary they must allow themselves to be surrounded, and must defend themselves to the last. A lost position has on many occasions been recaptured quickly thanks to the tenacity and heroism of a few machine gunners. In order to render such a desperate resistance possible, machine gun emplacements must fulfil the following conditions :—

(a) They must be surrounded by irregular barbed wire entanglements, made as invisible as possible.

(b) There must be several emplacements in case one should be rendered useless.

(c) The teams must be provided with protection against gas, and have plenty of food, water and ammunition.

3. *Lewis guns.*—The Lewis gun differs from the Vickers or Maxim by its greater mobility and its inability to sustain a rapid rate of fire for any length of time. Lewis guns should be used in a defensive line to economise infantry and to supplement the Vickers or Maxim guns of the brigade company, not to take their place. They can be used in co-operation with the machine guns of the brigade company to sweep depressions, covered approaches, &c., on which these guns cannot fire. Lewis guns fire over the parapet and can therefore often sweep ground invisible from a machine gun emplacement, which is usually sited near ground level and therefore has a low command. There must be the closest co-operation between the battalions and the commander of the brigade machine gun company over the choice of the positions and tasks for Lewis guns.

As Lewis guns are company weapons, their number in the front line will usually be determined by the number of companies holding it ; it may, however, occasionally be advisable to take the Lewis guns of supporting or reserve companies, if thereby the number of men in the front line can be reduced, and if those companies do not require their guns for other purposes.

Owing to the mobility of the Lewis gun and the absence of a fixed platform, emplacements, in the ordinary acceptation of the term, are not required. The Lewis gun can be fired off its light mounting over any portion of the parapet with very little preliminary preparation, and its fire can be brought to bear on an object very rapidly; a much greater liberty of action can therefore be allowed to this weapon than to the Vickers or Maxim gun. Although emplacements are unnecessary, definite "firing places" must be prepared, either by means of loopholes or in depressions in the parapet, defiladed from the front if possible.

In allocating Lewis guns to a portion of the defence, certain fronts should be given to them, and the teams should be thoroughly familiar with their "firing places," and the ground to be swept from each.

It is just as essential to keep Lewis guns under cover during a bombardment as it is to keep machine guns and their teams. In the case of the former weapon, however, as there are no definite emplacements, greater choice is possible in the selection of the spot for the shelters, provided the guns can come into action without delay.

40. *Action in Case of Attack.*

1. The measures taken by the defence to meet an attack have already been outlined at the end of Section 2 (p. 7). The main principles are :—

(*a*) To stop any attack from the outset by a concentration of artillery, machine gun, and rifle fire, the moment the enemy is seen issuing from his front trenches or collecting in them for an attack.* To this end careful arrangements must be made for observation and for communicating to the artillery by telephone or signal the moment the enemy's attack commences.

(*b*) It must be understood by all ranks that, should the enemy succeed in gaining a footing in our trenches, a counter-attack made at once, and without hesitation, will almost always be successful, even if made by inferior numbers. Counter-attacks by grenadier parties, especially from the flanks, are often particularly effective. On the other hand, if a counter-attack cannot be launched before the enemy has had time to organize and establish himself, then it becomes necessary to wait till an attack with adequate artillery preparation can be organized.

(*c*) Strong points and keeps organized for all-round defence must be held to the last, even though surrounded, and whatever happens to the rest of the line. They will

---

* A frequent method of attack by the Germans is to send on at first a few men only, and if they are successful to follow up with large numbers.

break up the enemy's attack and give time for a counter-attack in force to be organized.

(d) An attack on any large scale will be preceded by a very heavy bombardment, which may last several days and result in the partial obliteration of portions of the front system of trenches. During such a bombardment, special instructions may be issued by the higher commanders for the temporary withdrawal of the bulk of the garrison from portions of the front line. But strong points and localities organized for all-round defence must always be maintained.

2. All formations and units will have schemes made out for the defence of the portion of the line for which they are responsible. These schemes must always lay down the points of special tactical importance, which it is essential to hold. Arrangements should be made so as to be in a position to launch immediate counter-attacks, organized beforehand, to recapture any of these points which may be lost. If the important tactical points are correctly chosen, their re-capture should make untenable any intermediate portions of the line which may have fallen into the enemy's hands. As far as battalions and brigades are concerned, schemes of defence are based on the following principles :—

(a) The front system of trenches is the main line of defence. Should the enemy, following a heavy bombardment, succeed in penetrating into our line, he must be driven out immediately, before he has time to establish himself there, and our front system of trenches regained by counter-attacks directed against the points of tactical importance.

(b) It is the duty of the immediate supports, without waiting for orders, to reinforce the front line of trenches if required, and if any trench is captured to counter-attack at once without hesitation, and if any trench is blown up to occupy the crater at once, or prevent the enemy doing so by occupying our side of the crater and placing obstacles in the hole.

(c) The battalion reserve is to be used offensively to maintain the front system of trenches by counter-attack. Should the attack be on such a large scale that the battalion reserve is obviously insufficient to attempt the re-establishment of the line, it will be used to occupy a position to check any further advance by the enemy till a counter-attack by the brigade reserve can be organized.

(d) The brigade reserve will be used on similar principles to the battalion reserve.

The brigade scheme of defence will therefore include :—

(a) A definition of the sector for which each battalion in the front line is responsible.

(b) General instructions as to how the line is to be maintained in case of attack, with special reference to protection of the flanks should the enemy succeed in breaking the line to the right or left.
(c) The distribution of the machine guns of the brigade company, and the manner in which they are to be used.
(d) Arrangements for communication with the supporting artillery, to ensure fire being opened on the enemy's front line immediately.
(e) The state of readiness to be maintained by the brigade reserve, arrangements for instant communication of an alarm to it, and for its action.

The brigade reserve is usually in billets or shelters, one to two miles behind the front line. The defence scheme should arrange for it to move at once up to some position near the line of the battalion reserves by the routes most sheltered from enemy's observation and artillery fire. These routes must be reconnoitred by day and night by the brigade reserve, and guides must know them. While the brigade reserve is falling in, a mounted officer from it should go to brigade headquarters. The position to which the brigade reserve will be directed in case of attack, and the time it should take to reach it, should be known to battalions in front line. Arrangements to communicate with the reserve when it has reached this position must be made.

(f) Arrangements for action of any guns of the brigade machine gun company which are in reserve.
(g) Orders for first line transport.

Battalion defence schemes should include :—

(a) Arrangements for alternative methods of communication if telephone lines are broken.
(b) Action of battalion reserve, and arrangements for co-operation with neighbouring battalions in case of counter-attack by battalion reserves.
(c) Orders to officers in charge of strong points or keeps.
(d) Special arrangements for the action of grenadier parties, if necessary, and for keeping up the supply of grenades.

3. The precautions in case of an attack by gas are given in special instructions issued.

41. *Action of Artillery in Case of Attack.*

To meet a hostile attack by night, in a fog or under cover of smoke and gas, the important thing is to waste no time, but start the guns firing at once. Every gun should be normally laid on its "night line" (see p. 44) when not otherwise engaged, and, on receipt of a pre-arranged signal, will open fire at once on this line, "sweeping" a certain amount where necessary. The officer at the battery then endeavours to ascertain the situation, but, if the wires have been cut, he must use his own discretion as to continuing fire.

An alarm signal is necessary, and the occasions on which it should be used must be .clearly understood. Every precaution should be taken to prevent it spreading needlessly to neighbouring units. A visual signal, in case telephone lines are cut, must be pre-arranged.

It is advisable to test the alarm signal arrangements occasionally, but this should only be done by the brigade or division commander in consultation with the C.R.A. The telephone communications between the artillery and infantry should be frequently tested by day and by night, and at least once every 24 hours a round should be fired by the artillery, on a pre-arranged signal, to test the time taken between the sending of the message and the bursting of the shell.

CHAPTER V.

NOTES ON THE ATTACK IN TRENCH WARFARE.*

42. *Need for Careful Preparation.*

Success in an attack on a line of trenches depends on the training of the troops and on the thoroughness of the preparations made.

Confusion is apt to occur in any assault ; it is specially to be expected when attacking a maze of carefully prepared positions, and is the most frequent cause of failure. Unless it can be prevented or minimized by careful preparation and training, the enemy, whose counter-attacks will have been planned and be taking place over familiar ground, will probably succeed in driving the attackers back again.

Time for preparation is available, and full use must be made of this. The attack can, therefore, be said to begin weeks before the day fixed for the assault.

43. *Infantry Preparation for Attack.*

1. *Reconnaissance.*—Units in occupation of a system of trenches must always consider their line and the enemy's defences from the point of view of attack. Constant observation and patrolling will be required to add to the information available. The ground between the opposing front lines must be accurately reconnoitred so that no unsuspected obstacles, such as sunken wire or ditches, may hold up an assault. Every effort must be made to locate machine gun emplacements or strong points in the enemy's line, so as to be able to assist the artillery in the bombardment of the hostile defences. The whole of the enemy's system of defences over which the assault is to go must be made familiar to all ranks. A great deal of information is available from the excellent trench maps compiled from aeroplane photographs, and a study of the photographs themselves.†

2. *Plan of Attack.*—In the plan of attack the following are the chief points to consider from the point of view of infantry units (brigades and battalions) :—

---

* This chapter is not intended to be exhaustive and does not touch on very many most important preparations and arrangements which have to be made in the case of an attack on a large scale. It is intended to serve as a general guide as to the arrangements necessary on the part of brigades and battalions.

† The use of a magic lantern to throw aeroplane photographs on a screen has been found of great value.

(a) The distribution of the attacking infantry, *i.e.*, the number of lines or "waves" required for the attack, the points opposite which the assaulting lines must be strongest to deal with important objectives; the detailing of parties for special tasks ("clearing" parties, carrying parties, parties to dig communication trenches back to our front line, &c.). Definite objectives must be allotted to each body of men down to sections.

(b) The use of machine guns and trench mortars to support the attack, and arrangements to send forward a proportion of these behind the attacking infantry.

(c) The employment of grenadier parties

(d) The protection of the flanks, and arrangements for co-operation with, and assistance of, neighbouring units.

(e) Arrangements for communication.

(f) Arrangements for supply of S.A.A., grenades, tools, &c.

3. *Training.*—Before taking part in an attack, troops that have been a long time sedentary in the trenches will require special training to fit them for the assault. They will require marching and exercise to harden them. The enemy's defensive lines should be reproduced to actual scale somewhere well behind our lines, and the troops be practised in the assault, with and without officers, till every man knows his role in the attack. The co-operation of grenadiers with the rest of the infantry must be practised.

Signallers will require practice in visual signalling.

4. *Preparation of Trenches for Attack.*—All possible preparation of the trenches should be done long before the attack takes place, otherwise our intention to attack will be made plain to the enemy. Therefore in every system of trenches dispositions for an attack must be considered, and only minor additions should be necessary previous to the actual attack. It should be the aim of every commander to push his front line trenches before an assault as close to the enemy as possible, or at least to within 200 yards. This may be done by sapping and then joining up the heads of saps.

Advantage can sometimes be taken of a dark night and a new trench be dug in front of our old front trench during the night. In this case the party must be large enough to ensure getting cover the first night. This method will also only be possible if the troops holding the line, by stopping the enemy's patrols moving about, have established a superiority in the "debatable ground."

Assembly trenches must be prepared so that the successive waves of assaulting troops can be launched at the required time. These trenches should be prepared gradually. As far as possible use should be made of the existing trenches. A stereotyped form cannot be laid down for assembly trenches. The requisites are:—

(i) There must be easy egress both above ground and by communication trenches.
(ii) The assaulting troops must be close enough up.
(iii) The general line must be perpendicular to the line of advance.

In arranging assembly trenches care must be taken to provide forming up places for the various special parties, such as grenadiers, working parties, &c.

Sidings will probably be required for reserves. These can be suitably made off the "up" communication trenches.

Communication trenches must be provided in sufficient number to avoid congestion. One for up and one for down traffic per battalion frontage at least will be required, and between the last lines the number will require further increase, so that finally there will be one trench leading into the front line about every 50 yards.

Sign boards will be required on all communication trenches showing which are for up and which are for down traffic. Care must be taken to make those intended for evacuation of wounded wide enough and with sufficiently easy curves to allow a stretcher to pass.

Saps should be dug forward to be converted into communication trenches to the enemy's front line when captured. These should be tunnelled under the parapet, and when time allows be continued underground instead of above ground.

Exits from trenches must be prepared. These can either be made out of sandbags or by means of ladders. If ladders are used, all the ladders in one bay should be nailed together top and bottom by planks to prevent a ladder falling. Care must be taken that the tops of ladders do not protrude over the parapet.

In short, the preparation of trenches for assault entails the careful selection of the position of every man prior to the assault, and then the preparation of forming up places to suit.

Our own wire must be cut by parties detailed from the assaulting battalions. It should be cut during darkness the night before the assault.*

Bridges will have to be made over our trenches at certain points to provide for the advance of the artillery.

5. *S.A.A., Grenades, Food, Water.*—Stores of S.A.A., grenades, food, water, tools, and R.E. material must be established in the trenches. They must be conveniently placed for carrying forward to the captured position. One man should be in charge of each store. Special carrying parties will require to be detailed to carry the stores forward. Dumps of stores should be arranged in échelon, so that those in the trenches can be easily replenished.

---

* The fact that our own wire has been cut can be disguised by cutting transverse gaps or by écheloning the original wire thus ___ ___.

44. *Equipment.*

Assaulting troops should be as lightly equipped as possible, but it is difficult to reduce the weight carried below the following scale :—*

200 rounds S.A.A.
One day's rations (in addition to iron ration).
Two sandbags.
One pick or shovel to every third man.

Extra wire cutters, flares, smoke candles, etc., will be carried by a proportion of the men.

The equipment of grenadier parties is dealt with in the pamphlet on "Training and Employment of Grenadiers."

Grenadiers carry rifle and bayonet and 50 rounds S.A.A.

45. *Preliminary Bombardment.*

The artillery will prepare the way for the assault by battering the enemy's defences and destroying his obstacles. It will be the duty of the infantry to assist the artillery by continually reporting information gained about the enemy's line, and by observing the effect of the artillery fire mainly as to whether strong points or machine gun emplacements are being suitably dealt with, and the success or otherwise of the wire cutting. It is also necessary for infantry officers to make certain that they and the artillery commanders are in agreement as to the places where the wire is going to be cut.

This bombardment will probably take a long time, and during that time the garrisons of trenches should be reduced to avoid the casualties from the enemy's retaliation.

The enemy must be prevented from repairing his obstacles and trenches, after they have been damaged by artillery fire, by keeping the damaged portions under fire of trench mortars, rifle grenades, machine guns and rifle.

Definite tasks must always be allotted to trench mortars, in co-operation with the artillery.

46. *The Assault.*

The bombardment is kept up till the moment fixed for assault, when the artillery lifts, and the assault is launched.

The assaulting troops will consist of successive waves, each wave consisting of men extended at about one man every two yards, and with about 50 yards between waves. The number of waves will depend on the distance from our front trench of the final objective. The pace will be moderate, and on no account must a wild rush be allowed. The assault must be pressed on above

---

* Arrangements for storing packs of troops taking part in an attack must be made. Each man's name should be marked on his pack.

ground till its objective is reached, special parties being detailed to clear up the trenches over which the assault passes. These "clearing" parties accompany the assaulting waves, but remain behind in the trenches which they have been detailed to clear, while the assaulting troops press on to the final objective without entering them. "Clearing" parties will be composed largely of grenadiers.

The assaulting troops, on gaining the final objective, proceed to consolidate. R.E. parties and carrying parties to take up the tools and material required must be detailed beforehand. It may be impossible to take up material till after dark.

Parties must also be detailed to consolidate tactical points in rear of the assaulting troops, as they are gained. They will be assisted by the "clearing" parties, when these have finished their task of disposing of the enemy.

Generally speaking, then, attacking troops will consist of :—

(a) The troops detailed to carry through the assault to the final objective.
(b) The clearing parties who dispose of any enemy left behind in the trenches over which the assault has passed.
(c) The parties detailed for the consolidation of tactical points behind the assaulting troops and parties to carry up to the assaulting troops the material required to consolidate the positions won.

Special arrangements will have to be made, and special bodies of troops detailed to form a defensive flank on each side of the front assaulted, and also to attack isolated or semi-isolated strong points encountered on the flanks of assaulting troops.

The relative strength of the various parties cannot be laid down. They vary according to circumstances. The important principle is that every body of troops has a definite task assigned to it and knows what that task is.

47. *Action of Artillery during the Assault.*

At the moment fixed for assault, artillery fire must "lift" from the actual places to be assaulted, but must be kept up on the immediate flanks of the attack. Once the assault has been launched, the duty of the artillery is :—

(a) To keep down the fire of the hostile artillery. This is done by the counter-batteries.
(b) To prevent the enemy bringing up supports and reserves, by keeping up a steady fire on his communication trenches and other lines of approach and places in rear where troops might collect for a counter-attack.
(c) To give continuous support to the infantry during their advance and to deal with obstacles, strong points, &c., which may be holding them up.

The difficulties of this latter task are almost entirely those of observation and intercommunication. It is often impossible owing to smoke, dust, &c., to see exactly where the infantry have got to, and what is stopping their progress. The obtaining of timely information from the advanced troops presents great difficulties, and will depend largely on the efficiency of our counter-battery work. If the enemy's guns are not silenced, they will form a barrage behind our attacking troops which will make the sending back of information exceedingly uncertain.

The measures to be taken to ensure, so far as possible, continued artillery support to the infantry during the advance are as follows :—

(a) A proportion of field guns dug in close to our front trenches are useful to cover the flanks and give close support to the infantry.

(b) Battery commanders must place themselves where they can best see the general situation and keep touch with their batteries, and must be prepared to act on their own initiative, in the absence of information and orders from above.

(c) Each battery must have a forward observing officer, whose duties are to keep in touch with the infantry commander whom the battery is supporting, to keep the battery commander informed as to the exact position of the infantry, and to assist him in ranging on to anything that is checking the progress of our infantry.

The forward observing officer must be provided with telephone and signalling equipment. In selecting his position he must remember that his business is to assist the battery commander, not to join in the infantry fight, and that his information is of no use unless he can get it through to the battery commander. His best position will normally be the farthest point forward to which good communication has been opened up. He must keep the battalion commander informed of his whereabouts. It is then the duty of the infantry to let him know their requirements, and the measure of support they receive will depend largely on their reports being clear and intelligible to the artillery. For this reason it is very necessary that infantry officers should understand what information the artillery require.

Some form of light signal, visible to aircraft and artillery through smoke and mist, is required to let everyone know when the infantry have gained a certain objective. It should be sufficiently portable to be carried by every man. Flags and screens have been used, but they often get left behind and are then very misleading.

A proportion of light trench mortars should be brought up behind the infantry as soon as possible, and it may sometimes be possible to use them against some point which is checking the advance.

48. *Employment of Machine Guns.*

The role of machine guns in the attack is—

(a) To assist the artillery in the preparation of the attack, if required;
(b) To cover the assaulting infantry with their fire and to keep down flanking fire;
(c) To fill up gaps that may occur either laterally or in depth;
(d) To assist in the consolidation of the position and repulse hostile counter-attacks.

It is most important that all machine guns are allotted a definite task and given definite orders. The guns of the brigade company may be allotted as follows:—

(a) Some to cover advance by firing on the enemy's parapet, keeping down fire against flanks of attack, and sweeping ground in rear of enemy's first line, till masked by the advance of the infantry;
(b) Some to follow up the assaulting infantry. A proportion of these guns should accompany the parties detailed to consolidate tactical points in rear of the assaulting troops. Usually, Lewis guns only will go forward with the assaulting infantry at first. But some of the guns of the brigade company must be brought up as soon as possible after the assault has reached its final objective. These guns should not fire before the advance; the line of advance of each gun should be carefully selected beforehand;
(c) Some may be detailed to fire from positions in rear on points where enemy are likely to collect for counter-attack.

Lewis guns, owing to their mobility, are very suitable at the opening of an attack to provide covering fire from the front. Under cover of darkness, smoke, or artillery bombardment, Lewis gunners can creep out in front of the trenches and establish themselves in shell holes, ditches, long grass, &c., where it will be difficult to detect them. They may thus be able to cut wire which the artillery have been unable to cut and to fire on hostile machine gun emplacements, loopholes, and parapet.

Lewis guns will accompany the assaulting troops, but not in the first line, and will assist to keep down the enemy's machine gun fire, cover the re-organization of the infantry, consolidate the ground won, protect the flanks, and repel counter-attacks.

49. *Use of Grenadiers.*

Grenadiers will principally be employed in clearing trenches, after these have been successfully attacked, and also to check and destroy hostile bombing parties attempting to counter-attack.

They will be required to clear a portion of a trench from the flanks when its capture from the front has failed.

Full instructions on hand and rifle grenades and their employment are to be found in "The Training and Employment of Grenadiers." Emphasis may here be laid on the necessity of new units arriving at the front with thoroughly trained grenadiers, and also on the necessity for organizing with great care the supply of grenades during an attack.

50. *Communications.*

Buried telephone wires will previously have been installed in our front line system. These should be carried on up to the front line, and wire be ready to run across to the hostile line when captured. These wires will, however, be very exposed, and cannot be relied on.

Visual signalling and runners will therefore often be the only means available. The issue of discs, rockets, flares, or other improvised signals and their use must therefore be arranged. Receiving stations for visual signalling must be arranged for in our trenches, and these must be suitably protected.

APPENDIX A.

WINTER AVENUES.

(*Breastwork Communication Trenches.*)

1. The "avenue" shown in the figures 23–27 is primarily designed for construction in winter in ground where deep communication trenches are impossible and the difficulties of digging are increased by the soil clinging to the shovel and preventing a long "throw."

2. *Trace.*—The trace (fig. 23) is designed to reduce labour by combining protection from enfilade fire with passing places. A change of direction is made about every 60 yards to safeguard the avenue from being swept from end to end. Each arm is broken twice in its length at the passing places. These are made sufficiently wide to permit of stretchers passing the angles. The breaks are right-handed to enable a man to fire down the trench whilst keeping most of his body covered. In the arm nearest to the trench whence the communication starts, part of the inner breastwork of the passing places is omitted so that each section of the arm can be enfiladed from the parapet.

The avenues and borrow pits are flanked by means of short breastworks projecting from the elbows of the parapet.

3. *Profile.*—The profile is given in fig. 24. The height of the parapet will depend on depth below the surface of the ground at which the trench gratings will be clear of the subsoil water. Six feet of cover at least must be provided, and the more of this there is below ground the less the labour required for the parapet. But even if submerged, the gratings, being wired to the transoms, give a good foothold; and they can always be raised by putting another transom on the trestle, the parapet being heightened correspondingly.

A trench is, however, always advisable, even if the gratings are to be at ground level, as it acts as a drain and supplies some earth for the parapet. The sides of the trench should be revetted by slipping planks, brushwood or netting between them and the trestles, stakes being added if necessary.

The borrow pits should be as far as possible from the breastwork consistent with the power of "throw" in the particular ground. A 2-feet berm is the absolute minimum.

4. *Time of Construction.*—The avenue can be made in from 10 to 12 hours by two to three reliefs, and so can be completed in one night.

5. *Preparation.*—The most careful preparations must be made, materials calculated out beforehand, and transported to the nearest

convenient place under cover. There they must be laid out in such a manner as will ensure rapid and easy issue in the dark.

Working parties must be carefully calculated and divided up into small gangs.

The officers and men for each relief should be carefully practised by rehearsal by day, in their roles in the operations on which they will be employed.

It will hasten the work and prevent confusion if the avenue is started from both ends, and a stores dump is made at each of them.

It is generally inadvisable to extend a working party of 100 men from one point at night. The line of the proposed avenue should be divided into sections by marking stakes or other means, and each party led direct to its starting stake by its officer.

6. *Tracing and Reconnaissance.*—The R.E. should reconnoitre the ground at dusk on the preceding night, and mark out with tapes the lines along which the hurdles are to be placed.

If there is any danger of the tapes being observed by the enemy during the day, tracing must be done at dusk on the actual night.

The infantry officers in charge of parties should accompany the tracing officer and should familiarise themselves with the approaches to the dumps and starting points.

7. *Men and Tools and Materials.*—The men and tools and materials are as follows :—

First Relief (5 hours)—

	Per 4 yd. run.	Per 100 yd. run.
R.E.	2	50 (2 officers, 5 N.C.Os.).
Infantry	8	220 (5 officers, 20 N.C.Os.).
Shovels	8	220
Picks	8	200
Pliers	2	50
Measuring rods	1	25
3 ft. hurdles	4	100
5 ft. pickets	8	200 (3-in. diameter).
	(2 extra for first hurdles.)	
Wire (14 S.W.G.)	1,056 ft.	26,400 ft.
	(18 lbs.)	(450 lbs.)
3 ft. rabbit netting	8 yds.	200 yds.

Second Relief (5 hours)—

R.E.
Infantry } As in first relief.
Tools

18-in. hurdles	4	100
15-in. rabbit netting	8 yds.	200 yds.
Sandbags	70	1,750
Wire (14 S.W.G.)	264 ft.	6,600 ft.
	(4½ lbs.)	(112½ lbs.)

Third Relief—

	Per 4 yd. run.	Per 100 yd. run.
R.E.	2	50 (1 officer).
Infantry	4	110 (2 officers, 10 N.C.Os.).
Shovels	4	110
Picks	4	100
Trestles	3	76
8 ft. gratings*	1½	38
Planks for revetting	48 sq. ft.	1,200 sq. ft.
Mauls	½	12

Note 1.—The length of third relief depends on whether the full amount of digging has been carried out in the first and second reliefs. If the full amount has been done there is no necessity for a third relief, as the trench gratings can be laid by the R.E. next morning.

Note 2.—No mauls in first two reliefs on account of noise.

Note 3.—Reliefs are reckoned from time of leaving dumps.

8. *Organization of Working Party.*—The most convenient unit of organization is a squad consisting of two R.E. and eight infantry. This unit is completely equipped with tools and materials as in column 1, para. 7, and does 4 yards of avenue.

(a) Every five squads as above should be formed into an officer's party, with four N.C.Os. and four spare men, and does 20 yards of avenue, or just the length between the breaks (fig. 23), for which special squads could be provided if necessary.

(b) If the tactical situation permits, the infantry should leave their equipment at the dump,· and carry rifle and cartridge slings only.

(c) In the first relief each infantryman carries pick and shovel slung. Slings of spun yarn or cord should be attached to these beforehand by the party preparing the stores. In addition, a hurdle is given to every two infantrymen.

The two sappers carry the measuring rod, pliers, pickets, wire, and rabbit netting.

(*Note.*—Netting being in rolls would usually be carried down by the four spare men in every officer's party.)

(d) In the second relief four infantrymen in each squad carry the light hurdles and the other four carry the sandbags. R.E. carry the wire and netting (but see note to (c)). Tools are taken over from first relief on the ground.

9. *Extension.*—(a) A squad should march to its work as in fig. 27 (a).

---

* Special gratings for passing places to be calculated and 8 ft. gratings to be decreased accordingly.

The men are numbered and the hurdles lettered for purposes of reference.

(b) When the leading squad reaches the farthest forward end of the section allotted to the party, the hurdles are placed on the ground netting downwards and feet to the tape as in fig. 27 (b).

The men lay their arms 5 yards from the tape.

(c) The R.E. then measure the distances of the picket holes from the tape. The infantry then dig holes with the picks for the pickets and hurdle feet as in fig. 27 (c).

While the infantry are making the holes the R.E. prepare the wire.

(d) When the holes are complete, hurdle feet and pickets are put in them and the earth pressed down. (If the earth is so hard as to necessitate hammering, mauls must be brought and muffled, but only in circumstances of a very special nature must hurdles be mauled in, as the process strains them.)

(e) Nos. 1 and 7 then hold the hurdles, the R.E. put on the wires marked a and b in fig. 24 and the rabbit netting, assisted by the remaining infantry. The work will be greatly accelerated if the infantry have had previous practice.

(f) As soon as the netting and the ties marked a and b are fixed, the infantry are placed as in fig. 27 (d) and dig. While they are doing so the R.E. fix the other ties, and see that the borrow ditch is kept 2 feet or more as ordered from the netting stakes.

(g) When filling in the parapet, care should be taken to keep the weight of earth against the rabbit netting greater than that against the hurdles, in order to avoid forcing the latter over towards the trench.

10. *Tasks.*—In the first relief the number of cubic feet of earth in the parapets of the squads' task is 360 cubic feet (i.e., 4 × 6 ft. × 5 ft. × 3 ft.). This will be too much for the men to do in the time at their disposal after completion of wiring, etc., but they should be able to fill up to a height of 2½ feet.

In that case :—

Parapets = 300 cubic feet.
Two men in the trench dig 30 cubic feet each = 60 cubic feet.
Five men in borrow ditches dig 40 cubic feet each = 240 cubic feet.

In the second relief there are 60 cubic feet of the lower part of the parapet to be done (as above), and the top parts of the parapets amount to 210 cubic feet, a total of 270 cubic feet. This should easily be completed by the eight infantry in four hours, including filling the sandbags.

11. *Action of Reliefs.*—At the end of the first relief the infantry stand at their tasks. The second relief extend beside them and take over their tools. The first relief then put on their equipment and file off. Not until after they have gone will the second relief lay down their rifles and equipment.

R.E. hand over tools and duties in similar manner.

12. The work should be easily completed in one night *if careful preparations have been made*, and if not greatly interrupted by fire. Until the end of February a third relief is always possible before dawn. *It should be provided.* At the end of the first relief it can easily be seen if the third relief will not be required, and message to that effect sent.

APPENDIX B.

RAPID WIRE ENTANGLEMENTS.

The following are two methods of putting up wire entanglements, when rapidity is essential.

First Method (used by French).

Bays of wire fencing about 90 feet long are prepared beforehand, using light posts 7 feet 6 inches apart with horizontal top and bottom wires and diagonal wires (see fig. 28). For the top wire and one of the diagonals barbed wire is employed, plain wire about 0·15 inch thick for the others. Each bay is then rolled up and weighs about 90 lb.; it can be carried easily by two men if a stick is passed through it.

To put up the entanglement—unroll the bays along the front at 90 feet intervals and drive in the posts. This gives the front row of the obstacle (see fig. 28). In rear of it unroll and place more bays, zigzag fashion, so as to form a series of equilateral triangles with the original line. In this portion two rolls of fencing are required for each roll in the front row (see fig. 29). Repeat the same process to form additional sections.

Light posts are necessary from considerations of weight, but as there are three posts alongside each other where the straight and zigzag portions meet (except in the front and back row of fencing, when there are only two) a strong support is formed if the posts are bound together (see fig. 29).

Second Method.

See figs. 30, 31, 32, which sufficiently explain the method used.

As a variation of this method, work may be commenced by making the fence on the front line of posts first (work of Nos. 5, 6, 7, 8), then joining the first line of posts by criss-cross wires to the second (work of Nos. 1, 2, 3, 4, in fig. 29), and lastly making the fence on the rear posts. The advantage of this alternative method is that the working party then has the obstacle between them and the enemy the whole time they are working, instead of having to carry stores and work in the second stage in front of the obstacle erected by Nos. 1, 2, 3 and 4 in the first stage.

APPENDIX C.

ILLUMINATION OF OBSTACLES AND FOREGROUND.

The lighting up of the foreground and obstacles at night is of great importance.

The usual means adopted for this purpose is the Verys light, of which a liberal supply is now available, but occasions may arrive when the undermentioned methods will prove of value. These lights should be so arranged that they can be put in action instantaneously when the enemy approaches the obstacle : they must illuminate the whole of the obstacles and the foreground while leaving the defenders in shadow.

Bonfires.

Bonfires are effective when fuel is to be had. They may be built close to the line of the obstacle, with screens behind them.

A bonfire should be so built that it cannot easily be pulled down by the enemy. A stout post may be fixed upright in the ground, and the fuel built up round it in the form of a cone. Or three posts may be erected, three or four feet apart, with sticks nailed to them horizontally so as to form a cage, and the fuel piled inside. A heap of shavings or dry leaves should be placed at the bottom, and means of lighting arranged in connection with it. For this purpose a length of instantaneous fuze may be used, with one end in a small bag of gunpowder, under the heap of shavings, and the other inside the work. But the fuze must be kept in thoroughly good condition. Friction tubes form an excellent means of ignition. They can be fired by the release of a weight which is attached by wire to the eye of the pin. The tubes must be rigidly fixed, and strong wire used for suspending the weight. The blast from a friction tube being considerable, the end of the instantaneous fuze nearest the tube should be one inch away from it. Both ends of the fuze may be packed with quickmatch to ensure ignition. Another method is to arrange a match under the shavings so that by a pull on a cord the match will be rubbed against an igniting surface. The shavings must be enough to make a bright flame at once, and petroleum or pitch should be added to them if available. Materials for renewing the bonfire should be kept at hand. Small pieces of canvas should be fixed over the firing arrangements to protect them from weather.

Lights, Illuminating Wreck.

Lights, illuminating wreck are articles of store. They can be lit with either instantaneous or safety fuze. Instantaneous fuze should be stripped at the end to ensure good contact with the light. They illuminate a circle of about 100 yards diameter and burn for about 20 minutes.

Alarms and Flares.

Where night attacks may be expected, automatic alarms and flare light are useful adjuncts. They are usually combined with the obstacle. One of the simplest alarms is a row of tin pots, each containing a pebble, hung on a wire fence so as to rattle when the latter is disturbed. A piece of tin, 2 inches to 3 inches in diameter, such as the top of a jam pot, may be bent round the wire, and will answer the same purpose. Trip wires can be arranged to fire a rifle, or to fire a cartridge which, in its turn, will ignite a flare.

It must be borne in mind that flares lighted within a few yards of the perimeter of a camp, or close to a parapet, are difficult to screen effectively and are likely to be a source of greater danger to the defence than to the attack; they should therefore be used with great caution. At night troops have a tendency to concentrate their fire on any brilliantly illuminated area. A number of flares capable of burning from two to five minutes are preferable to one or two bonfires; a better effect is obtained from flares by placing them at some height above the ground. Convenient trees may be used for this purpose.

Arrangements for automatic alarm signals, in connection with entanglements or intermediate fences, generally have to be improvised on the spot with whatever materials are available.

A trip flare that has been found to work satisfactorily consists of a balanced board fixed in a trench having at one end the flare and at the other a heavy weight which is temporarily supported. The trip wire having been pulled, the support beneath the weight is withdrawn, and the end of the beam falls. By this means the flare appears above ground, and the jerk given to the beam fires a friction tube attached to the flare by instantaneous fuze, and so lights the flare. (*See* Fig. 33.)

The flare is composed of a mixture of nitrate of potash, sulphur and orpiment (Lights, G.S., long, Mark III).

Fig. 34 shows a similar device for the firing of a mine or bonfire outside the pit. A bonfire composed of straw, dry wood, &c., is readily set on fire by a small one-ounce cartridge composed of five parts white sugar and four parts chlorate of potash enclosed in grease-proof paper, fired by either instantaneous fuze or electrically by No. 14 fuze, with metal cap with the meal powder removed.

APPENDIX D.

INFANTRY AND ARTILLERY INTER-COMMUNICATION.

Apart from the unreliability of telephones, a difficulty, in the event of attack, is to ensure that a trained officer who can gauge the situation is at the infantry end. Infantry officers are liable at times to call prematurely for artillery support. Artillery are therefore on occasion perhaps slow in rendering the necessary assistance. Here the question of where the infantry end of the wire should be run to comes in. Some are against its being run into a fire trench, especially at night, for the following reasons :—

(a) The trench commander, who may be a junior subaltern, *thinks* he is going to be attacked, calls for artillery fire, and starts every gun in the Division firing. The whole Division is turned out unnecessarily and moral suffers. All commanders are short circuited.

(b) Wire run into a fire trench is constantly being broken. In case of attack it is almost invariably broken by the enemy's preparatory shell fire.

(c) The trench may be rushed and the instrument left in it. This has actually happened and the enemy may have listened to our messages until it occurred to somebody, some time later, to disconnect the wire at battalion headquarters.

Therefore it is best to run the wire to headquarters of battalions in trenches, or at furthest to a support trench well in rear.

The above is quite apart from the question of running a wire into an advanced trench for *observation* purposes, but here again there is a temptation to use it unnecessarily.

A better system at night is for an artillery officer, an orderly and telephonists to sleep at the headquarters of the battalion in the firing line. The former communicates with the battery by telephone *and* by orderly when the battalion commander requires artillery support. Artillery fire is immediately opened on the night lines while the officer makes his way to the observing station, connects up the communications with the battalion headquarters and the battery, and is ready to make alterations in the direction of fire when required.

Selection of battery position.—A battery which shows itself or allows its flashes to be seen at once comes under such a heavy and concentrated shell fire that any effective reply is out of the question, if, indeed, it is not put out of action entirely in a few minutes.

German artillery methods.—The Germans have a good system of observation, and trained observers with telescopes are constantly on the watch for any signs of movements in our positions and keep a special look out for artillery observing parties. Defilading from view of ground, observers must, therefore, take account of the highest ground in the enemy's position, although it may be distant.

Our infantry in support and reserve are apt to be very careless and often give themselves away, as the following extracts from a report show :—

(a) One morning I was coming away from a battery observing station. After crawling along a dirty ditch for some hundreds of yards, I came to some houses, where a few of our infantry were loafing outside their billets in view of the German high point, miles away. I warned them, but did not loiter in the vicinity. The billets were shelled the same morning.

(b) A few infantry showed on the skyline near one of our observing stations, which was promptly shelled.

(c) A battery commander incautiously showed himself at a window of the house from which he was observing. He was promptly shelled out of it.

It is most important that the enemy's notice should not be drawn to the localities in which the artillery observation stations are situated. Good observation stations are very scarce, and they are useful for the battalion commanders to view the hostile lines. No one should be allowed to go to the look-out place unless on duty, and then the greatest care must be exercised to get there unobserved.

Fig. 1.

Fig. 2.

Fig. 3.

DIAGRAM OF A SECTION OF A FRONT LINE, WITH SUPERVISION TRENCH, DUG-OUTS, AND SHELL TRENCHES.

Front Line Fire Trenches.

Fig. 4.

ALTERNATIVE ORGANIZATION OF A FRONT LINE.

Fig. 5.

TYPE OF STRONG POINT FOR FIFTY MEN.

Scale, 1″ = 32′

SECTION A—B.
Scale, 1″ = 16′

In bad soil it may be necessary to use Frames, or struts and walings in the magazines and communication trenches.

Fig. 6.

SUPPORTING OR STRONG POINT.

Portions a-b, c-d, e-f of Communication Trench enfiladed from S.P. as shown in dotted lines.

To increase fire effect trenches sloping gradually upwards may be constructed along dotted lines, as in section on m, e, f.

Fig. 7.

SECTIONS OF FIRE TRENCH.

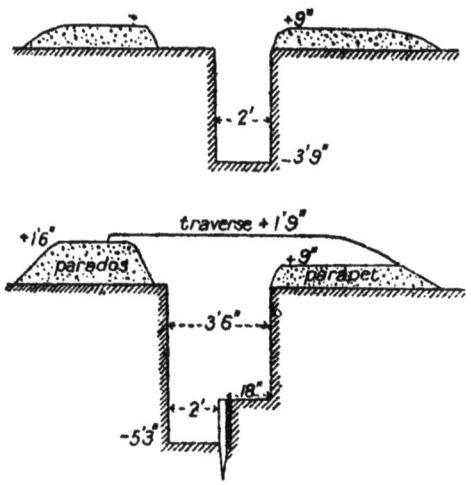

Fig. 8.

SECTION OF FIRE TRENCH IN WET SOIL.

Fig. 9.

BOMBING PIT.
Scale ½ in. = 1 ft.

PLAN.

SECTION ON A.B.

DEFENCE OF COMMUNICATION TRENCHES.

Fire trenches to defend communication trenches should be made as indicated below, rather than by widening the trench and cutting a fire step.

Fig. 10.

Diagram showing straight length of communication trench for protection against bombing and knife rests in position for blocking.

Fig. 11.

ALTERNATIVE FOR 30 YDS. STRAIGHT AT END OF COMMUNICATION TRENCH.

Scale 1 inch = 40 feet.

When the nature of the ground allows it, the following arrangement of the rear end of a communication trench may be substituted for the 30 yds. straight; it will generally be necessary to cut an inclined channel, running from ± 0 at the end of the loopholes L^1, L^2 to $-4'0''$ at B^1, B^2 in order to bring fire on the zig-zag portion of the communication trench.

Fig. 12.

TYPE OF SUNK WIRE ENTANGLEMENT.

Fig. 13.

FIG. 14.

WIRE ENTANGLEMENT.

SIDE VIEW.

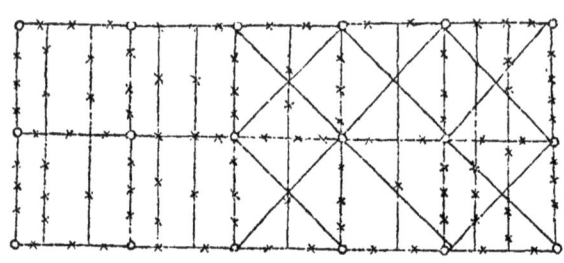

PLAN (WITHOUT LOOSE WIRE).

FIG. 15.

"KNIFE REST" OBSTACLE.

The efficiency of the obstacle is increased by adding barbed wire wrapped in loose spiral coils round it.

FIG. 16.

DUG-OUTS.

FRAMES.

Fig. 17.

TYPE OF DUG-OUT IN WET GROUND FOR EIGHT MEN.

Fig. 18.

MACHINE-GUN EMPLACEMENTS

of minimum dimensions as fixed by Commandant of M.G. School.

1. Emplacement with Overhead Cover, to fire Sitting.

Scale $\tfrac{3}{8}'' = 1'$.

PLAN.

SECTION ON A—B.

Fig. 19.

MACHINE-GUN EMPLACEMENTS
of minimum dimensions as fixed by Commandant of M.G. School.

2. Emplacement with Overhead Cover, to fire Standing.

Scale $\frac{1}{4}'' = 1'$.

PLAN.

SECTION ON A—B.

Fig. 20

MACHINE-GUN EMPLACEMENTS,

of minimum dimensions as fixed by Commandant of M.G. School.

3. Open emplacement, to fire Standing.

PLAN.

SECTION A—B.

Fig. 21.

MACHINE-GUN EMPLACEMENT.

Scale—$\tfrac{1}{8}'' = 1'$.

PLAN

SECTIONAL ELEVATION ON A—B.

Fig. 22.

TYPE OF MACHINE-GUN EMPLACEMENT WITHOUT PARAPET FOR USE BEHIND FRONT LINE.

This emplacement consists of two shafts, P and P', rectangular in section. The firing shaft P is $4'\ 3'' \times 2'\ 7'' \times 7'\ 8''$, and the entrance shaft P' is $4'\ 3'' \times 2'\ 7'' \times 10'\ 9''$.

These two shafts are $12'\ 6''$ apart and are connected by a shelter A, B, C, D, dug or mined, with a casing of $2''$ planks. One of the walls of the firing shaft P is provided with a recess $e, f, g, h, e', f', g', h'$, which serves for storing ammunition.

To fire, the machine gunner climbs up a ladder placed in shaft P and rests the machine gun on the natural surface of the ground.

There is no parapet, etc., showing above the ground, as the whole of the excavated earth is removed to a considerable distance. The emplacement is constructed away from any communication or other trench, and it is impossible for the most skilled observer to discover it.

Fig. 23.

WINTER AVENUE.

GENERAL TRACE.

Not to Scale.

A, B, C, D.—Points at which general direction changes.

p, p, p, p.—Traverses and passing places.

d, d, d.—Fire breastwork to cover, borrow ditches; 12 to 18 ft. long.

> Of same profile as Fig. 24, but no back parapet to give room for bombing.

e, e.—Returns left open to allow fire from reserve trench down the avenue.

Fig. 24.

WINTER AVENUE.

DETAILS OF PASSING PLACE.

Scale—$1'' = 2'$.

Fig. 25.

Fig. 26.

WINTER AVENUE.

DETAILS OF FLOORING.

Scale—$\frac{1}{2}'' = 1'$.

Should be covered with expanded metal to save wear and tear (and "fire").

TRENCH GRATING.

TRESTLE.

DETAILS OF HURDLES.

Scale—$\frac{1}{2}'' = 1'$.

LOWER HURDLE.

TOP HURDLE.

FIG 27.

WINTER AVENUE.
EXTENSION OF A SQUAD.

(a)

(b)

(c)

(d)

METHOD OF PUTTING UP RAPID ENTANGLEMENT.

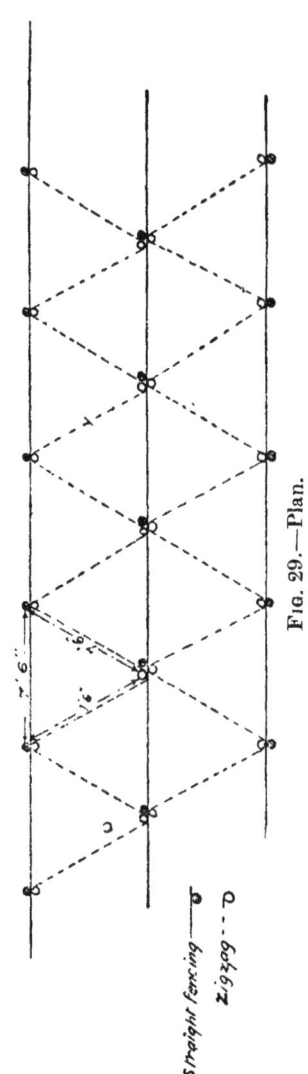

Fig. 28.—Roll Unwound.

Fig. 29.—Plan.

Straight fencing
Zigzag

Fig. 30.

METHOD OF PUTTING UP RAPID ENTANGLEMENT.

FIRST STAGE.

Fig. 31.

SECOND STAGE.

Fig 32.

COMPLETED ENTANGLEMENT.

Number of Men Required

2 to place stakes at proper point. (1 each side)
4 " drive in stakes (2 each side)
2 " wire Nº 1.
2 " " Nº 2.
2 " " Nº 3.
2 " centre wire Nº 4.
4 (2 each side) to wire Nº 5.
4 (" ") " " Nº 6
4 (" ") " " Nº 7
4 (" ") " " Nº 8
30 Total.

Plan
Setting out of Stakes.

Fig. 33.

AUTOMATIC FLARE LIGHT AND PIT.

a. Flare, composed of nitrate of potash, sulphur and orpiment.
b. Instantaneous fuze from flare to friction tube.
c. Friction tube.
d. Balanced plank carrying flare and weights.
e. Prop stick connected to trip wires.
f. Trip wires.
g. Weights.
h. Lugs.
i. ¾ round bolt to form hinge.
j. Quick match around friction tube.
k. Pliable wire to fire friction tube.

PLAN

Fig. 34.

FLARE PIT.

Section

Plan

REFERENCE.

a. Friction tube placed so that pull comes at a right angle.
b. Quick match.
c. Instantaneous fuze to flare.
d. Prop stick.
e. Guide stake.
f. Pivotted arm 2′ 6″ × 2″ × 2″.
g. Weight attached to arm and connected by flexible wire or spun yarn to friction tube.
h. Flexible wire or spun yarn.
i. Flexible wire or spun yarn from prop stick to weight.
k. Weight connected by flexible wire or spun yarn to prop stick and thence to wire "l."
l. Wire connected to "cut" or "trip" wire.
m. Wire pin through two uprights and acting as pivot for arm on which weight "g" rests.
n. "Cut" or "trip" wire.

INDEX.

A.
	PAGE
Advanced posts, occupation of	14
Alarm signal for enemy's gas	38
„ „ in case of attack	55
Ammunition, loose, including fired cases, to be collected	39
„ supply and storage of	40, 58
„ taken into trenches	36
Arms, standing to, before dusk and dawn	39
Assault, preparations for	6
Assembly trenches	57
Attacks, means of assisting	6
„ hours when usually made	38

B.
Bayonets, fixing of	38
Blankets, not to be taken to the trenches	36
Bombing trenches, function and siting of	16, 22, 40
Breastworks, design of	23, 28
„ where used	15, 23
Buildings, preparation for defence	32
Burster layer	23, 29

C.
Cellars, preparation of, for defence	18, 32
Communication trenches	7, 17, 58
„ „ design and number of	25, 26, 40, 64
„ „ preparation for flank defence	27
Companies to be self-contained	49
Concrete	31
Counter-attacks, immediate attacks desirable	52, 53
Craters to be occupied	53

D.
Dead, disposal of	45
Defence, measures employed by the	7
Drainage of communication trenches	26
„ of trenches	31
Dug-outs, site of	25, 28
see "Shelters"	

E.
Entanglement, wire	15, 27, 40
„ „ rapid	68
Entrenching tool, need for practice in use of	19

	PAGE
Equipment carried in attack	59
„ wearing of, in trenches	38

F.

Flooring of communication trenches	26
„ of trenches	20, 24, 31
Fuzes of enemy's shell to be sent to artillery	45

G.

Garrison, distribution of	48, 49
Gas, alarm signal to be arranged	38
Grenades, storage of, in trenches	40, 58
Grenade-throwing	9
Ground-sheets to be taken to the trenches	36
Guides on relief of trenches	35, 36, 37

H.

Headquarters not to be changed unnecessarily	47

L.

Latrines	17, 31, 45
Lewis guns	51, 52, 62
Lime, chlorate of, to be kept in each trench	31, 45
Listening posts	7, 34, 38, 40
Locality, defended (*see* "Strong points"), definition of, and organization for defence	17, 18
„ garrison always to be maintained	53
Log-book, trench, need for	34
Loopholes	25, 32, 33, 42

M.

Machine guns	49, 50, 51, 62
„ siting and design of emplacements	16, 18, 30, 50, 51
„ to be loaded and in position at night	38
„ company, O.C., to reconnoitre line before taking over	35

N.

Night lines for artillery, selection of	44, 54

O.

Observation, arrangements to be made for	41, 52
„ stations	7, 25
Obstacles	15, 27, 40
„ design of	27, 68
„ need for construction of	19

	PAGE
Officers of a company not to live in one dug-out	38
" on duty in trenches	38
" to visit artillery observation stations	45
Orderlies, use of	46, 47
Overhead cover not to be used in fire trenches	25

P.

Packs, care of, during attack	59
" when taken to the trenches	36
Parados	20, 22, 24
Parapet, undercutting of, forbidden	28
Parties for carrying stores to be detailed from troops in rear	39
Periscopes	25

R.

Rations for forty-eight hours to be taken into the trenches	36, 39
Ration parties to be armed	39
Reliefs, hours to be varied	35
Reports to be rendered of completion of relief	37
Reserves, action of	53, 54
Reserve line, design and siting of	16, 20
" function of	16
Revetting of communication trenches	26
" of trenches	20, 22, 23
" training of men in	41
Rifles to be inspected twice daily	39
Rifle batteries, fixed	43
Rubbish to be buried	45

S.

Salients, advantages and disadvantages of	12
Sandbags, advantages and disadvantages of	23
" earth for filling of	40
" method of laying	24
" to be available ready filled	24
" to be carried by relieving troops	36
Schemes of defence, to be prepared	53
Sentries, in trenches	38
Shelters, bomb-proof and splinter-proof	28, 29, 30, 40
Shoemakers, in battalions	46
Signalling, visual, to be arranged	46
Signposts, to be provided	26, 40, 58
Slit trenches, functions and design of	16, 29, 33
Snipers	9, 25, 41, 49
" relief of	34, 43
Socks, dry, to be carried	46
Staffs, to remain till relief of trenches is completed	37

	PAGE
Standing orders, points which should be embodied	36
Stores, lying about to be collected	39
„ trench	34, 37
Strong points, garrisons always to be maintained	53
„ „ in trench lines	16, 17, 18
„ „ to resist to the last	52
Supervision trenches, functions of	15
Support trenches, functions of	16
„ „ siting and design of	16, 20, 25

T.

Tactical points, occupation of	12
„ „ ability to recognize	13
Telephone lines, civilians to be arrested if seen touching	47
Time, to be obtained from the signal service	47
Tracks, visibility to aircraft	13
Traverses, design and construction of	21, 22
„ in communication trenches	26
Trenches, design of	6, 7, 10, 12, 20, 22
„ relative advantages of forward and back positions	11
„ siting of	10, 12, 13, 15
Trench feet, precautions against	46

V.

Villages, defence of	18
Very lights, to be handed over on relief of trenches	37

W.

Whistles, not to be used in gas alarms	38
Wind, direction of, to be reported	47
Working parties, numbers available	41
Workshops, brigade, forming of	39

www.ingramcontent.com/pod-product-compliance
Ingram Content Group UK Ltd.
Pitfield, Milton Keynes, MK11 3LW, UK
UKHW021904240426
12048UKWH00045B/641